Contents

Foreword

United Kingdom industry and the public sector are under ever increasing pressure to take account of the environmental implications of their processes and products. The Confederation of British Industry has argued in *Narrowing the gap: environmental auditing guidelines for business*, that environmental auditing must become an essential corporate strategy through which businesses can reduce their impact on the environment and improve their competitive position in the market. In the public sector, many local authorities have produced environmental charters and environmental auditing, a more fundamental review of the environment and the authority's role in protecting and enhancing it is a logical next step.

Furthermore, both the British Government and the European Commission are adding to the pressure for environmental auditing, the former through legislation such as the Environmental Protection Act 1990 and the latter through draft regulations on eco-auditing. The Commission also has plans to extend the role of environmental impact assessment to policies and programmes, improve the enforcement of EC environmental legislation, and extend rights of access to environmental information.

The development of these strategies at international, national, local and corporate level indicates the importance attached to protecting the environment and ensuring high quality service for citizens and customers.

The British Library is in a unique position to help the development of environmental auditing through the provision of timely and pertinent information. As part of a series on the environment, the Library's Science Reference and Information Service has launched a number of guides to key environmental issues, the most recent being *Environmental information: a guide to sources*; *Environmental auditing: a guide to best practice in the UK and Europe*; and *BS 7750: what the new environmental standard means for your business*. This new guide to environmental auditing is an appropriate successor combining the practical knowledge of a number of environmental consultants and experts with the unique information skills of staff in the Library's Environmental Information Service.

The guide is fully indexed, and most of the documents cited are available through the British Library Science Reference and Information Service in London, or the British Library Document Supply Centre at Boston Spa in Yorkshire. The databases mentioned in the text can all be searched on behalf of customers by staff in the British Library Environmental Information Service (071-323 7955).

A Gomersall, Director, The British Library, Science Reference and Information Service, 25 Southampton Buildings, London WC2A 1AW. Tel: 071-323 7485.

1 Introduction

About the *Guide*

Environmental auditing is not a new discipline. In America it has been in existence for 20–30 years, although its emergence in Europe is more recent. In Britain, it is becoming increasingly well established, with larger companies leading the way in demonstrating the benefits of being seen to assess their environmental liabilities.

The chapters in this book are based on papers which were originally given at a course entitled Environmental Auditing: how green is your business? organised by the British Library and held on March 10th 1992.

The British Library's Environmental Information Service noted a significant increase in the number of enquiries it was receiving on environmental auditing, particularly from small and medium sized companies. The course was developed to give this group a practical introduction to the issues involved.

The contributors to this book are all experts in their field, with experience of environmental auditing on a practical level, or experience of the associated legislation or literature. The delegates to the course were from a wide range of industry sectors. Their questions and the speakers' answers are included with the appropriate chapter. The editor has sought to retain something of the individual style of each contributor so that each chapter reflects the particular style of personal presentation.

What the *Guide* contains

There are many definitions of environmental auditing or as they are often called, environmental reviews. In Chapter 2, the editor examines some of these definitions to provide a clearer view of what environmental auditing includes.

In Chapter 3 John Smith, of Groundwork Environmental Review Services, provides an overview of the environmental auditing process. He focuses in particular on the benefits an environmental audit can bring to a management system and discusses how economic savings can be made in terms of reassessed manufacturing methods, saved waste disposal costs and rationalised usage of resources. The chapter also examines the marketing advantages of being seen as a greener company, and the significant benefits of staying within the law.

Environmental auditing is set to become increasingly important as a result of the changing legislative framework. In Chapter 4 Dr Albert Mumma of Simmons and Simmons in detail at the liability and law aspect of environmental auditing. He covers the Environmental Protection Act of 1990, the British Standard 7750 on environmental management systems,

1

the Water Resources Act of 1991 and the draft EC Eco-Audit Regulation, and many related aspects, such as Integrated Pollution Control, BATNEEC (Best Available Techniques Not Entailing Excessive Cost), and contaminated land.

As the market expands the increasing interest in green audits has been reflected in the growing number of environmental consultants operating in the field. Many companies are interested in finding out how to do an audit with consultancy help, or using their own staff, and the course had two speakers who were able to give advice on the practical details involved in carrying out an audit. In Chapter 5, and Chapter 6, Mark Hadley of Environmental Auditors Ltd. and Ted Allett of Environmental Resources Ltd. (two of the most well established environmental consultancies in the UK) discuss getting started, and what the auditor needs to know. These chapters analyse what an environmental audit is, the types of audit currently in existence, how the audit is carried out and how to choose an auditor.

Once an environmental audit has been completed it is important to find ways to continue reaping the benefits. Krystyna Krajewska and Paul Ingrams of Greenmantle discuss how to do just that in Chapter 7. Greenmantle is a green marketing company with plenty of experience in helping clients to understand why the results of their audit should be publicised. This is an important aspect, as many companies have discovered that it is not worth carrying out an audit without making the results public.

In Chapter 8 the editor, Helen Woolston discusses the most important sources of information available for those who want to find out more about environmental auditing, green policies and legislation. This chapter provides information on the key printed and online sources and on relevant organisations to contact for advice.

Chapter 9 provides a reading list with full bibliographic information on all the key documents discussed in the book.

Finally the index provides a quick and easy means of locating information on the organisations, databases and specific environmental auditing topics covered in the guide.

Helen Woolston (December 1992)

2   Defining the terms

What exactly is meant by the term 'environmental audit'?

There is a lot of confusion, about exactly what an environmental audit is and how it can be applied in different situations. Other terms have appeared for types of environmental audit or for related practices. This chapter outlines and defines the various terms currently in existence.

Basically, an environmental audit is a system that checks for policies and practices which can improve corporate environmental performance. During an audit a number of evaluation methods may be used, such as: reviewing procedural documentation; visiting the site; and using interviews and questionnaires.

The standard *Oxford Dictionary* definition of an audit is that 'it is an official systematic examination of accounts'. The phrase came from the financial world but environmental auditors have modified the definition to cover the whole field of environmental science. The International Chamber of Commerce have produced a good, all embracing definition, which has received a fairly wide acceptance amongst auditors and industry.

> 'Environmental auditing is a management tool, comprising a systematic, documented, periodic and objective evaluation of how well environmental organisation, management, and equipment are performing with the aim of helping to safeguard the environment by:
>
> i)   facilitating management control of environmental practices;
>
> ii)   assessing compliance with company policies, which would include meeting regulatory requirements.'

This has been adopted by the EC in their Eco-Audit Regulation proposal document. In the draft Regulation document, the EC says that 'Environmental audit includes determination of the factual data necessary to evaluate performance'.

Other definitions from the EC Eco-Audit proposal include the following:

> ' "environmental review" means an initial comprehensive analysis of the environmental issues, impact and performance related to activities at a site.
>
> "environmental policy" means a statement of a company's overall aims and principles of action with respect to the environment.
>
> "environmental statement" means a statement prepared by the company in line with the requirements of this Regulation.'

What's in a name?

Many terms are bandied about in the realm of environmental auditing, but they are all based on an assessment or review of a management system with regard to its environmental performance. While an environmental audit is basically a checking process, a phrase which is now used more frequently is 'environmental review'.

Environmental review is used to describe the process of collecting data, rather than checking it against certain criteria. A review is usually the first step undertaken by a company or organisation starting the environmental audit process. It helps the company to set down what their operations are, and to list their suppliers, products and wastes. This can then lead on to an environmental audit proper, where the results from the review are checked and a forward plan of action devised.

Other frequently used terms include 'environmental assessment' or 'environmental impact assessment'.

The meaning of the phrase *'environmental assessment'* has changed over the last few years. Previously it was used to describe situations in which no particular standards existed against which to carry out an audit. Now, it is widely used as either an alternative to the term 'environmental audit', or as a global term to cover the whole auditing/review process.

Environmental impact assessment involves study into the likely environmental impact of a proposed development – such as a new road, building or landfill site – or of a proposed action. It is very much concerned with determining the likely future impact of a new operation on a site or community.

The phrase *'environmental management systems'* is closely associated with environmental auditing. To comply with the new British Standard 7750 on environmental management systems companies will have to (amongst other things) conduct an environmental audit. BS 7750 describes environmental management systems as 'the organizational structure, responsibilities, practices, procedures, processes and resources for implementing environmental management'.

Types of audit

Environmental audits can be subdivided into various types according to what the company is evaluating. Companies need to ensure they have carefully considered the scope of the audit (the systems to be evaluated) during the first stage of the auditing process.

Systems to be checked can include corporate policy, systems analysis, operational procedures and practice, level of emissions, production of waste, use of energy, transport systems, training procedures and emergency procedures. The main types of audit are:

- *Liability (pre-acquisition) audits.* When a company is about to buy a site, it needs to check out the land and buildings with regard to any future environmental liability it may take on as the new owner. The value of a site will vary according to the presence of any contamination, and once this is established, the purchase price may change to reflect the cost of clean-up under the contaminated land regulations of the Environmental Protection Act 1990.

- *Compliance (technical) audits.* These are used by companies to check that they are complying with set guidelines, which can include current environmental legislation, or company policy.

- *Product audits.* According to what a company wants, this can involve looking at the supply, production and distribution processes involved in the life of a product. This may include quality assessment of the whole system, and can look onwards to the marketing of the product.

- *Environmental management audits.* This type of audit looks at whether the company has an environmental policy in place, and can advise on writing one. It will look at the management structure of a particular site or a whole corporation.

Further details on the types of environmental audit currently in use are given throughout this book.

No doubt new terms and definitions will continue to evolve as environmental legislation and regulations develop further. For any extra help with defining the terms, ring the British Library Environmental Information Service on 071-323 7955.

3 Introduction to the benefits

John Smith, Groundwork Environmental Review Services, Fairstead, 8 Latchmoor Avenue, Gerrards Cross, Buckinghamshire. Tel: 0753 883537

John Smith was seconded to Groundwork Environmental Review Services after many years working in industry, most recently for BP.

The Groundwork Foundation was set up by the Department of Environment, with local authority and local business help, to bring about environmental regeneration in partnership with the local community and voluntary organisations. The network has been operating for a decade, through local Trusts.

The Groundwork Environmental Review Services have been specially designed for medium and small firms.

This chapter includes the following:

- Environmental pressures on business.

- Why are audits needed?

- Objectives of a review.

- The Groundwork checklist.

- Stages in a Groundwork review.

- Benefits of environmental audits.

Environmental pressures on business

Pressures on business can result from many things, including new legislation and the economic climate. Five years ago, most businesses hoped that the environmental issue would disappear, but it has not, it has simply gained more importance. In fact it is now possible, in some cases, for businesses to lose their licences to operate, if they do not stay within the environmental laws. The main environmental pressures on business are summarised in *diagram 1*.

Diagram 1

> ### ENVIRONMENTAL PRESSURES – AN OVERVIEW
>
> New regulations – New standards or stricter enforcement of regulations can raise pollution control costs.
>
> Higher effluent and waste disposal costs – General waste disposal costs are rising fast and some wastes will become very costly to dispose of.
>
> Products – Environmental pressures affect product manufacture and use, packaging, recycling and disposal.
>
> Siting – New investments may fuel delays and lead to higher costs.
>
> Clean-up – Companies must assess whether they can clean-up current and prior damage.
>
> Incidents – E.g. Sandoz, Exxon Valdez, Union Carbide's Bhopal.
>
> Issues – Companies must avoid sensitive issues such as damaging rain forests, hardwoods, ozone layer, porpoises, etc.

New environmental regulations affecting business include the Environmental Protection Act 1990, the British Standard 7750 on environmental management systems, and the European Community's proposed Eco-Audit Regulation. At this stage, introduction of the latter two will be voluntary, but companies who are seen to be putting them into action will certainly achieve a better environmental reputation.

Both BS 7750 and the EC Eco-Audit Regulation set out standards for a company to follow when assessing, checking and updating their environmental management. It is these UK and EC auditing initiatives which make it imperative that companies begin to undertake a review of how their policies and processes affect the environment.

BS 7750 was published in April 1992. It specifies quite clearly the systems needed to secure improving environmental performance within a particular company.

At the European level, plans for the Eco-Audit scheme were announced on 20 December 1991, the adoption of regulations is due in the second half of 1992. Although voluntary at this stage it could become mandatory later on once the procedure has been reviewed. The procedures will allow for common standards and a common system of auditing within the various member states. The attraction for industry, or for a particular site is that if the Eco-Audit scheme is taken on board voluntarily, they can actually achieve certification and an Eco-label, which can be used on products coming from that specific site.

From April 1993 onwards there will be a new register of contaminated land, put together by local authorities. Appearing on the register could affect the collateral of a piece of land, due to high clean-up costs. Prospective purchasers of a piece of land will need to take into account any clean-up costs for which they will be responsible and which may reduce the purchase price.

Companies can expect standards to be more strictly enforced in the future by bodies such as the National Rivers Authority, who will pass on higher effluent and waste disposal costs.

Recycling, including the recycling of product packaging is likely to become increasingly cost effective. German legislation states that manufacturers must make arrangements for the return and disposal of their own packaging. The pressure from consumers who wish to use recycled products, and to have their domestic waste recycled has grown considerably.

Environmental issues will have an increasing influence on companies' investment decisions. New investments which require environmental impact assessments are likely to be subject to close scrutiny.

As well as legislative pressures, public pressure has also increased due to incidents such as the Exxon Valdez, Sandoz and Union Carbide. There is increasing concern and more active campaigning on issues such as the depletion of the tropical rainforests, use of non-sustainable hardwoods and the depletion of the ozone layer.

Think globally, act locally is a phrase which was introduced by Friends of the Earth and has achieved great significance. Pressure groups are encouraging more people to think in the long term about the fate of the planet, while helping to change things by improving their immediate surroundings.

Groups pressurising businesses

There is increasing pressure on business to become 'greener'. These pressures come from a number of sources:

- Investors – shareholders concerned about good management and liabilities.
  A company will be pressured by its investors and other stakeholders to do well economically. This success can often be linked to having a good environmental reputation, as well as keeping within the environmental legislation. An example of environmental pressure on business was reported in an article in *The Times*, of Tuesday 14 January 1992. This was called 'Clean-up costs force banks to rethink lending' and said 'if we lend to companies who are not going to be in business because of environmental issues, that will not be of benefit to the bank or its customers'.

- Employees – concerned about recruitment issues and company ethics. Company employees frequently initiate environmental practices within their own firms, even if it is something as simple as organising a collection for paper to be recycled. A management which can be seen to introduce good environmental practice will impress their workforce, who will probably have enthusiastic new ideas. New graduates looking for jobs will also be favourably impressed by a company working for the environment.

- Neighbours – concerned about the community, the company's relationship with regulatory authorities and its future expansion and new sites.
  The population which lives and works near a factory site will be the first to influence a company's green image. Various chemical plants in Teeside for example have had to contend with continued high level publicity either because local residents have discovered they are suffering from pollution-linked diseases, or because they have protested about the pollution of their environment.

- Consumers – concerned about quality linkage and supplier audits. Consumers are taking increasing account of the environmental character of products. The increase in green advertising and marketing over the last two years has resulted in an increase in the purchase of environmentally friendly goods. However, those companies making false green claims were very quickly found out, and this reflected badly upon them, to the detriment of their reputation.

- Suppliers – suppliers may have to change their product and process specifications.
  Now, as well as needing to ensure a quality green product and accurate green marketing, companies need to ensure that their whole operation relating to that product is environmentally sound. This extends to using suppliers who comply with environmental requirements.

- Media – the media are increasingly reporting on environmental achievements.
  A scan of a national quality paper on any day is likely to produce an article on how environmental pressures are affecting businesses. Details of those winning environmental awards are widely publicised and companies sponsoring conservation projects are frequently mentioned.

Why are audits/reviews needed?

Groundwork prefers to use the term *environmental review*, rather than 'audit'. Larger companies are, on the whole, comfortable with the auditing concept but many small and medium-sized companies are resistant, even to the name. Environmental reviews provide a useful starting point. Once a company has conducted a review it can develop or refine its company environmental policy and then audit its performance against that.

Audits/reviews are needed to help companies stay competitive and within the law in an increasingly 'green' business world. They need to be conducted in the face of:

- Greater environmental awareness – Public and employee awareness of environmental performance is increasing, and the ability to assess and improve this will benefit the company.

- Legislation (see chapter 4) – There has been a growth in UK and EEC environmental legislation. Now more than ever companies need to be environmentally aware to stay within the law.

- Advanced technology – Companies wishing to remain within the new law of Integrated Pollution Control will turn to cleaner technologies, which in turn will result in more efficient systems.

- Medical research, e.g. sick building syndrome, COSHH, dangerous products register.

- Limitation of resources – There is a growing realisation of the need to use sustainable resources and to dispose of wastes in an environmentally friendly way.

At the moment, environmental management is not in place in most British businesses. An environmental review can be a useful first step in helping a company to introduce proper environmental management. It can highlight for the company the key technical and managerial problems to be addressed. The main management and technical issues are summarised in *diagrams 2 and 3*.

Diagram 2

ENVIRONMENTAL MANAGEMENT ISSUES

Leadership	Policy, accountabilities, standards, rules
Training	Management, staff, contractors
Procedures	Operating, maintenance, inspection
Planning	Emergency preparedness
Incidents	Reporting, investigating, analysing, controlling
Auditing	Proactive monitoring
Engineering	Design and change controls

Diagram 3

ENVIRONMENTAL TECHNICAL ISSUES

Exposures	Hazardous substances	Products, wastes
	Sources of release	Plant and equipment
	Sensitivities	Physical, political, visual image
Standards	Regulations	
	Company standards	
	Plant design/operation	Containment
Measurement	Emissions	Air, ground, water
	Integrity	Corrosion
	Methods	Sampling/analysis
Evaluation	Acceptability	
	Action levels	
Control	Treatment	Separation, Filtration
	Transport and disposal	Landfills, incinerators
	Restoration	Grading, seeding
Data	Substances	

The main steps in an environmental audit are summarised in *diagram 4.*
The diagram shows the importance of securing management commitment
at the beginning of the environmental review/audit process. It also shows
how a review serves as an important first step in the audit process.

Diagram 4

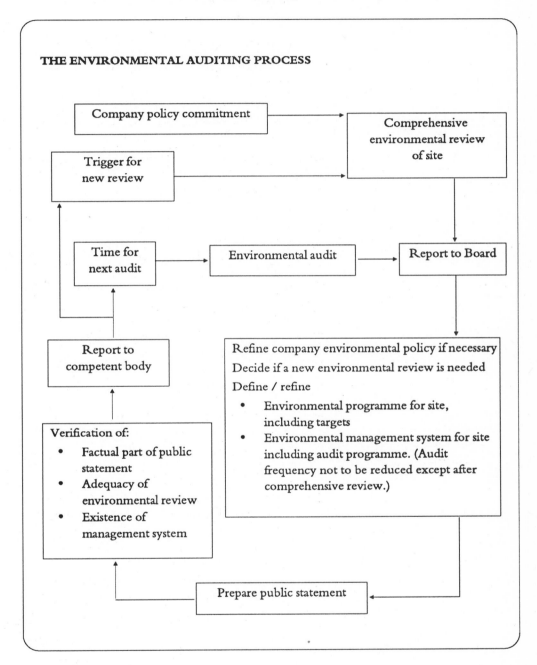

THE ENVIRONMENTAL AUDITING PROCESS

Company policy commitment → Comprehensive environmental review of site

Trigger for new review → Comprehensive environmental review of site

Time for next audit → Environmental audit → Report to Board

Report to competent body

Refine company environmental policy if necessary

Decide if a new environmental review is needed

Define / refine

- Environmental programme for site, including targets
- Environmental management system for site including audit programme. (Audit frequency not to be reduced except after comprehensive review.)

Verification of:

- Factual part of public statement
- Adequacy of environmental review
- Existence of management system

Prepare public statement

Objectives of a review Groundwork has developed a number of key review objectives which are:

- To assist in developing environmental policies and management systems within the context of current and future legislation and standards.

- To provide findings to management to support the development of effective environmental improvements.

- To promote greater environmental awareness within the company. Lower and middle management often get very keen, and come up with money-saving ideas for the company.

- To encourage the company to improve communications with the community, through improved environmental performance.

An environmental review can look at people, equipment or materials, but often they concentrate on the latter two. Reviews should also consider the life of the product after it has left the factory and moved into the community. The first three steps a company must establish are:

- *Policy* – Companies must have achievable goals and be able to communicate them to employees, investors, suppliers and the public.

- *Strategy* – A clear strategy is necessary if goals are to be achieved in terms of the organisation's responsibilities, priorities and resources.

- *Programme* – Manageable targets must be set which include procedures, training and budgets.

The Groundwork checklist Groundwork has developed a checklist of 12 main elements as an aide memoire. This takes the form of a list of questions which could be asked, to get people thinking along the right lines:

- Environmental *policy*, is there one? Who is responsible for it?

- Has the company briefed itself on the relevant *legislation and regulations?*

- Does the company offer any *environmental training* or *environmental awareness development?*

- How does the company deal with its *contractors?* Are they trained in environmental practices?

- Are there plans in place to deal with *accidents and emergencies?*

- How good are the internal *communications* (and external, with trade associations)?

- Which *materials* are used by the company? Are they screened for environmental friendliness?

- Is there a written policy for *plant design and process?*

- How does the company deal with its *energy* usage?

- Does the company carry out any *environmental pollution control and monitoring?*

- How environmentally friendly are the systems for *transport, distribution and storage?*

- How can the *site management* be improved with regard to the environment?

In the majority of reviews, companies save money by introducing energy saving systems and developing good practice.

Stages in a Groundwork review

These are six main stages in a Groundwork review.

- *Scoping* – Before the review team is sent in, a scoping exercise should be carried out. The Managing Director should be interviewed to assess the general scope of the review.

- *Planning* – The audit process should be planned with the Managing Director, using the aide memoire (detailed above).

- *Information gathering.*

- *Interviews* – Employees should know about the environmental policy. It is vitally important for the auditor to listen to the answers, as well as to ask the right questions.

- *Preparation of a draft report and discussion of priorities with the Managing Director.*

- *Training* – Various accidents have occurred due to a lack of good training, or to poorly briefed contractors. It is important to assess whether contractors have been as well trained as the permanent staff and whether lessons have been learned from any accidents, emergencies or near misses.

Benefits of environmental audits

The benefits of environmental audits are clear and wide ranging, they include:

- To provide a means of targetting strengths and weaknesses.

- To allow targeting of resources.

- To allow progress monitoring.

- To aid comparison between operations and/or plants.

- To help identify cost saving opportunities, including waste minimisation.

- To assure that an adequate database exists.

- To help to reassure the Authorities.

- To facilitate cost effective insurance.

- To raise employee awareness of environmental issues.

- To ensure key issues are focused on, e.g. training.
- To allow credit to be given for good environmental performance.

Questions

Question 1

To what extent will Germany's packaging legislation be applied, will it go right down to details like butter wrappings?

Answer

It does not provide for domestic waste, but for example, petrol stations will need to provide drums for collecting waste oil.

Question 2

Environmental auditing can sound like a system designed to save labour. Are there any pressures from unions against this?

Answer

Unions in the UK have shown a great interest and involvement in environmental auditing. The Trades Union Congress and individual unions are developing policy documents to help their members.

4 Environmental legislation: UK and EC laws

Dr Albert Mumma, Simmons and Simmons, 14 Dominion Street, London, EC2M 2RJ. Tel: 071-628 2020

Dr Albert Mumma completed a PhD on environmental law at Cambridge University in the summer of 1991. He currently works in the environmental law department of solicitors Simmons and Simmons, where his work covers all aspects of British and EC environmental law. He also coordinates the production of the Simmons and Simmons bi-monthly *Environmental Law Newsletter* providing useful up-to-date information on recent developments in environmental law.

This chapter considers:

*   Current UK legislation.

*   Current EEC legislation.

Introduction

To keep up with the changes in environmental legislation which affect what UK businesses can or cannot legally do it is essential to keep an eye on the developments in the USA and European Community. Environmental auditing is a process of establishing and determining good practice within a company, with regard to its environmental impact. A serious environmental audit will involve several stages and will take some time to complete. It is vital to know what state the legislation will have reached when a business has finished its environmental auditing process. Without this knowledge the compliance part of the audit will be overtaken by events, and it will be expensive to repeat and update. The key is to anticipate the legislation and to stay ahead of it.

UK legislation

This section deals in detail with the Environmental Protection Act of 1990 and the Water Resources Act of 1991. *Diagram 5* on page 22 summarises the features of these key acts.

Environmental Protection Act 1990

Integrated Pollution Control

Integrated Pollution Control (IPC) was introduced by Part I of the Environmental Protection Act 1990. It covers around 5,000 particularly polluting and complex industrial processes. From 1 April 1991 new and substantially modified processes have to comply with the IPC requirements. Existing processes also have to comply but on a rolling timetable running from 1 April 1991 to 1996. Once a process is brought under IPC it may only operate after receiving an authorisation from Her Majesty's Inspectorate of Pollution (HMIP).

IPC has two key principles: Best Practicable Environmental Option (BPEO) *and* Best Available Techniques Not Entailing Excessive Costs (BATNEEC).

1)   Best Practicable Environmental Option (BPEO)
Industry must apply the concept of Best Practicable Environmental Option to discharges from its processes. Companies must look at the the impact of their activities on the environment. The impact should provide the most benefit or least damage to the environment as a whole, at an acceptable cost, in the long term as well as the short term.

The environment has three media: land, water and air. Before the introduction of the Integrated Pollution Control mechanism it was not important for businesses to judge which of the three media would best absorb the discharge. If a decision was made to discharge to water, and the particular regulatory authority had granted consent, that was fine even if disposal on land offered a less damaging option.

HMIP has been charged with the duty of balancing the impact of discharges on the three media, to see which medium would best absorb any particular discharge. The concept has been implemented in legislation and the first applications were made in April of 1991. By August 1992, 91 authorisations had been granted, in relation to combustion plants, gasification and petroleum processes.

For existing processes, determining the BPEO requires an audit of their environmental practices. For new processes, a continous audit would assist in ensuring that the process continues to meet the requirements of BPEO principles.

2)   Best Available Techniques Not Entailing Excessive Cost (BATNEEC)
BATNEEC requires that the Best Available Techniques Not Entailing Excessive Costs be used to prevent the release of prescribed substances into the environment. Where total prevention of pollution is not practicable, BATNEEC requires that these techniques be used to reduce the release of

such substances to a minimum, and to render harmless any substances which are released.

The problem is that there has at no stage been an adequate definition of 'excessive cost'. The definition tends to vary. In times when environmental issues are top of the agenda, then no cost is considered excessive. This is an issue of discretion, a view shared by HMIP.

However, the key point in BATNEEC is the question of *techniques*, which involve the entire range of the company's operations:

- The process used, i.e. its concept, design and components, including the way the components are connected together to make the whole.

- How that process is operated.

- Staff numbers.

- Working methods.

- Training.

- Supervision.

- The manner of operating the process.

The role of environmental auditing in meeting the requirements of the best available techniques then becomes clear. It is only through a regular environmental auditing mechanism that a company is able to determine whether or not, for instance, its staff numbers are adequate for a particular process. For this reason, it is important to be aware that environmental auditing is not just a policy principle.

The Duty of Care: Section 34

Section 34 of the Environmental Protection Act 1990 has imposed the Duty of Care on those who, in one capacity or another handle controlled waste. This Duty applies from 1 April 1992, to all those who handle controlled waste, unless they are specifically exempted.

'Duty of Care' is a legal requirement that producers, or those handling waste, at any stage of the waste chain, have a Duty of Care, or a shared responsibility to ensure that controlled waste is:

- Not managed illegally by others who have to handle it subsequently (this refers to anybody in the waste chain).

- Adequately secured so that it does not escape from control.

- Transferred only to an authorised person.

- Adequately described to enable proper handling and treatment, e.g. hospital and domestic waste. (The management of clinical waste differs entirely from the management of domestic waste, which means the description of the waste must be accurate. It is a criminal offence to give a misleading description of the waste.)

The Duty applies to all handlers of controlled waste, this includes all those who:

- import
- produce
- carry
- keep
- treat *or*
- dispose of controlled waste.

It does not apply to householders in relation to their own domestic waste, but it does apply to controlled waste, which is limited to household, commercial or industrial waste. It does not extend to explosives, waste from a mine or a quarry or agricultural waste.

The Duty of Care cannot be delegated to another person. At the same time it is not intended to be absolute. That means a waste handler is entitled to show that he has handled the waste reasonably, by fulfilling criteria based on reasonableness. For instance, the waste handler may hand over the waste to a person who, he has reasonable cause to believe, is competent to handle the waste safely. The categories of person to whom waste may be legally handed over are:

- A local authority with power to take waste (e.g. a waste collection authority. Currently the provisions require local authorities to privatise their waste disposal activities.)

- A registered waste carrier. (Waste carriers need to register with effect from April 1992.)

- A carrier who is exempt from registration. (An example is a person who is transporting waste he has himself produced. If someone transports their own waste rather than someone else's, they are exempt.)

- A licensed waste manager. Local authorities, in their capacity as waste regulatory authorities are required to give waste management licences. This will come into effect from 1 April 1993.

- A waste manager who is exempt from registration requirements.

The Duty of Care will be enforced by a criminal penalty of up to £2,000 in a magistrates court, and an unlimited fine in the Crown Court. Companies will need to audit their operations to see that they comply with these particular requirements.

The Department of the Environment published a Code of Practice on the Duty of Care in December 1991, setting out what is expected of companies.

Contaminated land registers

Section 143 of the Environmental Protection Act 1990 contains measures designed to provide the public with information on the whereabouts of potentially contaminated sites. It also grants powers and imposes duties in relation to the clean-up of contamination and the reduction of soil contamination in the future.

With regard to public information, each local authority has a duty to compile and maintain a register of land 'subject to contamination'. This is defined as land which is being, or has been put, to contaminative use. 'Contaminative use' is defined as any use of land which may cause it to be contaminated with noxious substances. The local authorities were initially expected to have the registers ready for inspection from 1 April 1993. Although this timetable will not now be met the Government published a consultation paper and draft regulations on 31 July 1992 for implementing this provision.

There are 8 categories of contaminative use which would lead to an entry in the register. The register itself will be split into two parts: A and B. Part A will record land which has not yet been investigated and/or treated while Part B will record land which has been investigated and/or treated. However, treatment will not by itself lead to the removal of an entry from the register.

One of the most pressing issues in relation to contaminated land registers arises from the possibility of blight following entry in the register. A company will find an environmental audit of its activities a useful way of determining whether they pose a risk or have already caused soil contamination which might ultimately lead to a listing on the register.

Personal liability

Section 157 of the Environmental Protection Act 1990, and section 217 of the Water Resources Act 1991 have introduced personal criminal liability on those in charge of the operations of the polluting companies. They provide as follows:

> 'Where an offence under any provision of this act committed by a body corporate is proved to have been committed, with the consent or connivance of, or to have been attributable to any neglect on the part of any director, manager, secretary or other similar officer of the body corporate or a person who is purporting to act in such a capacity, he as well as the body corporate shall be guilty of that offence and shall be liable to be proceeded against and punished accordingly.'

A company has here an added reason, if one were needed, for carrying out an environmental audit: to ensure that its activities comply with the regulatory requirements, so that it does not expose its senior officers and directors to the risk of personal criminal liability. In 1991, two directors in Yorkshire were charged with the offence of pollution in a river, after their company was declared insolvent.

Clean-up powers

Regulatory bodies have clean-up powers which enable them to enforce the clean-up of sites which have suffered pollution.

These powers are concentrated in four different authorities.

1) Her Majesty's Inspectorate of Pollution (HMIP)

HMIP has powers under section 27 of the Environmental Protection Act to go in and clean-up a site and then charge the operator of the site with the costs of the clean-up.

However Part I of the Environmental Protection Act was only implemented in 1991 and HMIP has yet to exercise these powers.

2) Waste Regulatory Authorities

From April 1992 Waste Regulatory Authorities have had powers which are very wide in scope. The powers relate to waste disposal sites that are found to be contaminated or that present a threat of pollution to the environment. In such an instance, the waste disposal authority may go in, clean-up the site and charge the owner of the site with the costs.

It is quite likely the owner of the land will not be the same person as the one who deposited the waste there perhaps 20 years earlier. The importance of this is in relation to people who intend to acquire land. When land is acquired that is either contaminated, or presents some particular threat to the environment, the owners will be charged, even if they are not the perpetrators.

3) Waste Disposal Sites

Section 61 of the Environmental Protection Act 1990 places upon the Waste Regulatory Authority (WRA) a duty to inspect its area to detect whether any land is in such a condition by reason of 'the relevant matters' affecting the land that it may cause pollution of the environment, or harm to human health. The 'relevant matters' to be addressed are:

> 'the concentration or accumulation in and emission or discharge from the land of noxious gases or noxious liquids caused by deposits of controlled waste in the land'.

The authority can enter and inspect any land where controlled waste has been deposited or where it has reason to believe that there may be concentrations or accumulations of such gases or liquids. Once such land has been identified, the authority has a duty to take whatever steps appear reasonable to it in order to avoid pollution or harm. The cost of such works can be recovered from the person who is currently the owner of the land, except for any costs which the person can show were incurred unreasonably.

It should be noted that the original disposers have no liability under Section 61, unless they are still the owners. If they are operating the site under a waste management licence but are not the landowners, other remedies may be available to the WRA, but not under this Section.

4) National Rivers Authority

The National Rivers Authority has powers under Section 161 of the Water Resources Act 1991, to clean-up water pollution and charge the person responsible for the pollution with the costs.

In Spring 1992 there were actions taking place in the courts which were of interest in this respect. For example, under the rule of Rylands v. Fletcher, the Cambridge Water Company claimed damage for pollution of water supplies by two tanneries. The company tried to recover £1 million from the tanneries for the contamination clean-up cost. The Cambridge Water Company lost the case in the High Court on the grounds that the spillages from the tannery had occurred in the 1960s, but had stopped by 1976. The EC Directive which set standards for drinking water was produced in 1980. The Directive would have affected the particular borehole in question after 1980, but before this time there was no law in place which the spillage would be contravening.

The Company appealed and the result was reported in the *Financial Times* on 25 November 1992. Three Court of Appeal judges awarded £1,046,866 against Eastern Counties Leatherwork Ltd. to the Cambridge Water Company in compensation for contaminating the aquifer.

The judges found that the fact the pollution was unforseeable made no difference to liability. This is a very significant decision, as it is the first time a party has been found liable for historical pollution.

Statutory Nuisances

Part II of the Environmental Protection Act tidies up the legislative provisions on the powers of local authorities to prevent nuisances occurring on land. The Act contains a consolidated list of items which constitute a statutory nuisance and gives the local authority power to take action in anticipation of the nuisance occurring. Under the new provisions a local authority, when satisfied that a statutory nuisance exists or is likely to occur or recur, can serve an abatement notice requiring the abatement of the nuisance or prohibiting or restricting its occurrence or recurrence.

The provisions relate, among other things, to 'any accumulation or deposit which is prejudicial to health, or a nuisance' and can therefore apply to land with a potential for contamination. They also relate to premises that are in such a state as to be prejudicial to health or which constitute a nuisance.

The local authority can recover any expenses reasonably incurred in abating or preventing the occurrence of a statutory nuisance. These can be recovered from 'the person by whose act or default the nuisance was caused and if that person is the owner of the premises, then from him'. The costs are a simple debt, which that particular authority would then seek to recover in the normal way, including auction of property.

The significance of these clean-up powers is that, whereas before, the consequence of pollution was simply a £2,000 fine after a court hearing, now there is the possibility, in fact an increasing likelihood, of companies being required to bear the costs. The costs will probably run into millions.

Diagram 5

SUMMARY – UK LEGISLATION

UK legislation has been changing very fast. There are two key legislative instruments to keep in mind.

The Environmental Protection Act of 1990
The Water Resources Act of 1991

Both Acts have fundamentally changed the scope and reach of environmental control.

There has been a significant change in the depth and sophistication of the legislation and that is perhaps the key change. Most of these ideas have been around for a long time. What has changed is the emphasis and the sophistication of the legislative provisions, and it is because of that sophistication that companies will feel significant effects.

The changes in UK legislation fall into three categories:

1) New areas of environmental control. The Government has introduced strict environmental control over matters that were previously not specifically controlled. The most significant include:

   Integrated Pollution Control
   Duty of Care in waste management
   Contaminated land registers

2) Stiffer penalties. When the law is broken stiffer penalties can now be imposed, not just on the companies themselves, but on those individuals, such as Directors, or other senior officers, who are in charge of the company's operations. This imposition of *personal criminal liability* is a very interesting shift in the law. The trend now is to look at who is in charge of the operations, and to make them criminally liable.

3) New powers for regulatory authorities. Regulatory authorities such as the National Rivers Authority (NRA) and Her Majesty's Inspectorate of Pollution (HMIP) are now empowered to carry out works remedying pollution or threatened pollution and to recover the expenses from those responsible for the pollution.

Before these new provisions there was a tendency to say 'this river has been polluted, a fine of £2,000 must be paid' and that was that. Now under the new provisions there are not only fines, but the polluter is also told to clean up the pollution. If it is not cleaned up, the relevant regulatory authority can do this and charge the bill to the original polluter. Whereas fines were only £2,000, clean up costs can go into millions of pounds, a different issue altogether!

EC legislation

The European Community is more active than ever in the environmental arena with some very interesting developments.

The European Community always tends to start by proposing the most stringent measures possible before modifying them. It is easy to think that these proposals are too extreme, but they serve as useful indicators of EC thought.

The EC proposals initially follow developments in the United States. So it is possible to get a good idea of where the United Kingdom will be in three or four years time by monitoring EC and US developments.

Diagram 6 on page 27 shows the areas covered by EC environmental legislation.

The proposed Council Directive on packaging and packaging waste

The European Commission formally adopted on 15 July 1992 a draft Directive on packaging and packaging waste which is now before the Council.

The draft Directive arose from what is popularly known as the 'Danish bottles case'. Denmark had decided to introduce legislation, requiring any beverages marketed in Denmark to be marketed only in returnable bottles. Those using other bottles could no longer be marketed in Denmark. However, that caused an instant barrier to trade, since all European Community beverage producers who did not sell drinks in such bottles were barred from trading in Denmark. A repeat situation has now arisen in Germany, which has said that particular products can only be marketed if particular packaging requirements are met.

Because the European Community is, as a rule, a free trade market, the Danish case went to court. The European Court of Justice ruled that the environmental benefits of the Danish law outweighed the barrier to trade but ruled against Denmark because Denmark's requirements were too restrictive. The EC had meanwhile produced a Beverage Containers' Directive (85/339/EEC), partly in response to Denmark's laws on beverage containers.

Once that had happened, people in the beverage industry felt that they were being singled out against other packaging producers. Consequently, the European Community has now introduced a draft Directive, which aims to set out a legal framework for minimising and as the proposal would hope, finally eliminating, unnecessary packaging.

The draft Directive has the following objectives:

- To reduce the impact of packaging waste on the environment.

- To encourage a reduction in the consumption of raw materials and energy.

The Directive is to cover all packaging placed on the market and all packaging waste whether released at industrial, commercial, office, shop, service or household level. To achieve the target and objectives set by the

Directive, Member States were initially required to meet the following objectives:

- To attain a 'standstill' of packaging waste at the 1990 levels of packaging consumption. It is estimated that the 1990 per capita consumption of packaging was 150 kilograms. So in the year 2000 it would still be 150 kilograms.

- That no later than five years after this Directive comes into force at least 60% of the packaging waste would be recovered and 40% should be recycled. In ten years time, they would want to see 90% recovered, 10% recycled. This is moving towards a situation where there is no packaging waste.

- To take measures to minimise the presence of noxious and hazardous substances in packaging.

In order to comply with the targets, the Directive proposes a number of measures, including:

- The establishment of schemes to ensure return of used packaging by the consumer.

- The establishment of economic instruments to ensure the provision of sufficient funds to run management schemes for returned packaging.

- The establishment within the packaging industry of standardised packaging for products to facilitate re-use.

- The promotion of the concept of waste recycling and providing information on schemes available to the public to recycle their used packaging.

The draft also has proposals which are qualitative in nature:

- Limiting excessive use of packaging material.

- Reducing packaging volume and weight to the minimum adequate amount for safety and consumer product acceptance.

- Limiting the presence and concentrations of heavy metals, inks, dyes, pigments, adhesives, etc. in packaging material.

- Ensuring packaging waste processed for composting is of a fully biodegradable nature.

This draft met with stiff criticism, and certain proposals have been dropped. These include:

- The 'stand still' provisions on packaging waste plus the five year deadline for achieving interim targets for recovering, recycling and final disposal of packaging wastes. However the ten year deadline remains.

Nevertheless, even with those provisions dropped, the proposed packaging Directive will have a far-reaching impact on packaging and packaging waste. Companies will need to audit their activities to ensure that they do not fall foul of the requirements as it will not be possible to sell products which do not meet the requirements.

The proposed landfill Directive

This proposed Directive was produced because the Commission perceived a need to harmonise landfilling practices across the EC. It is important that a uniform standard of environmental protection is established, to prevent waste for landfilling being shipped across Europe to member states where protection is lax.

Because of the environmental hazards that are now emerging as a result of the mis-management of old landfills, the Commission wants to set a high standard to prevent any further soil and water contamination, and to prevent whole sites becoming unusable. The proposed Directive stresses that landfills should be seen only as the final option for waste disposal and that greater emphasis should be placed on recycling and reclamation. This is in order to avoid those problems, largely related to soil and groundwater contamination, which arise from landfilling waste. The risk to the environment from landfill waste should be minimised by treatment where appropriate, prior to landfilling, and dumping or uncontrolled disposal must be eliminated.

While the Commission regards landfilling as a final resort in waste management, in the UK over 90% of controlled waste finds its way into landfills. The Commission is also against the British practice of co-disposal (which the Commission refers to as 'joint disposal'). Co-disposal is the practice of landfilling industrial and hazardous waste in the same landfill with municipal and domestic waste. If waste is to be landfilled at all the Commission prefers that it is dumped in different landfills according to its category.

The Commission sees cost as a mechanism of the proposed Directive, to ensure that landfilling is not seen as an easy, cheap option. Article 16 states that all costs involved in landfilling should be included in the price charged by the operator, from the cost of the land right through to closure, after-care and insurance costs. Other provisions in the proposed Directive which will make landfilling an expensive option include:

- Requiring the operator to provide a financial guarantee to cover the estimated cost of closure procedures and aftercare operations of the landfill.

- Requiring the setting up of an 'after-care' fund which would cover the expense of any operations which might be necessary to prevent or cure environmental damage caused by disposing waste to a landfill. The fund will be charged according to the class of the landfill and the type and tonnage of the waste landfilled.

The proposed environmental auditing Regulation

Environmental auditing is seen in the European Commission not just as an internal management mechanism, but also as a means of informing the public about the effects of a particular company's activities on the environment.

The idea is not just for a company to inform itself and to improve its own operations, but also for the public to know the results of the environmental audit.

As it currently stands, the proposed Eco-Audit Regulation has three objectives:

- The establishment and implementation by companies of internal environmental protection systems aimed at achieving high levels of environmental protection.

- Systematic, objective and periodic evaluation of environmental performance of such systems.

- Informing the public on environmental performance (Article 1(2)).

The proposed regulation requires that companies registered under the scheme:

- Carry out an environmental audit of sites registered under the scheme.

- Prepare an environmental statement based on the eco-audit results.

- Have the statement validated by an accredited environmental verifier.

- Submit the validated environmental statement to the relevant authorities.

- Keep the statement at the disposal of the public.

The scheme is currently voluntary and therefore companies are under no obligation to register sites under it. However, in view of the information and other benefits that arise from an eco-audit, companies will find it a worthwhile exercise, even where the company does not register under the EC scheme. It is particularly useful in helping investors make informed investment decisions.

Diagram 6

> **SUMMARY – EC LEGISLATION**
>
> On the EC front, developments have been a little more rapid. In five or six years time, up to 90% of UK environmental laws will have been brought in from the European Community.
>
> This means the position of the European Community on any issue is now even more important than Whitehall's.
>
> There are three important pieces of legislation to concentrate on:
>
> 1) Proposals on packaging and packaging waste. These are likely to revolutionise the entire approach to packaging and while they have not yet been approved, such approval will soon be given.
>
> 2) Proposals on landfill of waste. (These are of particular concern to the UK.)
>
> 3) Proposals on environmental auditing.

Questions

Question 1

You mentioned that the EC dislikes landfilling, but do they suggest an alternative?

Answer

It is not the practice of the EC to suggest alternatives. One major alternative is incineration, but incineration is just as contentious. Greenpeace and Friends of the Earth for example do not support incineration. The Commission does not suggest a particular alternative, they simply say don't use the landfilling method.

Question 2

The initial reaction in the UK to BATNEEC was that finally the European Community had come round to the UK way of thinking. They have accepted that what are needed are flexible, technological controls like Best Practicable Means (BPM). Is there any difference in interpretation between Best Practicable Means and BATNEEC?

Answer

Yes there is. The difference in interpretation lies in the importance placed on cost. BPM was the predecessor of BATNEEC. In BPM, cost is more of a consideration than in BATNEEC. BPM was thus more flexible and cost factors were given more weight.

Question 2 (cont.)

Under BPM there was far more discretion given to the Alkali Inspectorate at that time.

Answer

BATNEEC also includes room for discretion but there is a stronger leaning towards published standards and arms length control, than there was under the BPM system.

Question 3

Are there any laws or proposals regarding the emission trading permits in use in the United States?

Answer

Not specifically, but the European Community has a policy paper on economic issues generally, and emission trading is considered, but they haven't yet drafted a particular proposal to introduce emission trading. It may be under consideration somewhere in the background. The European Community does not give very much advance notice of what is being considered.

Question 4

Will BATNEEC be slowed down, due to lobbying?

Answer

Because operators are concerned that their own process would be unduly crippled due to the costs of a particular requirement they spend time lobbying. There is an argument going on now involving the power producers, PowerGen, who want to introduce a particular process and do not want to install special technology. Although the technology is available, and has been proven, the argument is that this would be unnecessarily expensive.

BATNEEC incorporates an element of discretion in the phrase 'not entailing excessive costs'. The discretion of the regulatory authority is in interpreting what 'excessive costs' means. It is difficult to have an objective prior standard about this, it will have to be worked out in practice. In contrast best available technology is a more objective standard, as it is easy to accept and to agree on what is the best available technology.

The economic burden BATNEEC places on companies as well as pressure from the European Community will determine how quickly the standard is adopted. The element of discretion within BATNEEC makes it a very flexible standard, some say that this flexibility renders it meaningless, whilst others argue that it is the element of discretion that will make it workable and effective.

5 Environmental auditing: getting started

Mark Hadley, Environmental Auditors Ltd, Devonshire House, 164 Westminster Bridge Road, London, SE1 7RW. Tel: 071-439 0246

Mark Hadley is a Council member of the Institute of Environmental Assessment, and Managing Director of Environmental Auditors, an environmental auditing consultancy. He is therefore directly involved in keeping up environmental auditing standards, and has much experience in the auditing field.

This chapter considers the following:

- Types of environmental audit (including what an audit is, and how it is applied in various situations).

- Components of an audit.

- Contaminated land (how auditing can be used to evaluate contaminated land).

- Benefits of environmental audits.

- How to choose an environmental auditor.

Types of environmental audit

There are many different types of audit which can cause confusion for those new to environmental auditing. However, audits can be divided into two broad types: product and corporate audits, see *diagram 7*.

Product audits

A product audit looks at:

- Assessing or reassessing quality assurance programmes – how to actually produce a product in an environmentally benign way.

- How the raw materials making up the product are resourced.

- How consumer information on products is appraised before it is sent out.

- How the product will impact on the environment, and on consumers.

- How that particular product is packaged.

- The ease of product disposal, when it has passed its useful life.

- What the effects of the product were during its actual use.

Diagram 7

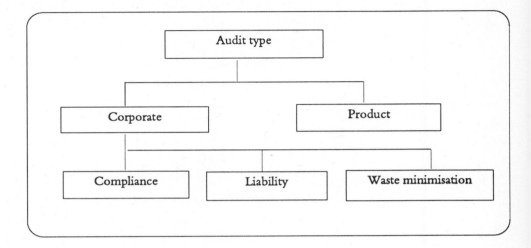

Corporate audits

Within companies environmental management systems are going to be increasingly important. The new British Standard 7750 on environmental management systems will have a fairly dramatic impact on the UK industry over the next few years. An audit is an integral part of BS 7750 and can be used quite simply within it.

Corporate audits can involve looking at:

- A single site.

- A single company.

- An operating division (most common in large companies).

- An environmental management system.

Specific audits within the operating divisions include:

- A purchasing audit which analyses how they resource and buy their raw materials and what impact that has on the environment.

- A transport systems audit which examines their effect on the environment.

Corporate audits can be divided into compliance, liability and waste minimisation audits. This division reflects the different ways that environmental auditors are actually approaching the problem, and how they are applying their services.

a) Compliance audits

Compliance (or technical) audits check whether a company is complying with environmental legislation, the environmental regulations under which it has to operate its day to day business and with the company policy.

Many companies are moving towards an approach in which they write their own company environmental policy, develop an implementation plan for that policy and then find a system to audit the effectiveness of that policy within their company, or at an outside level.

b) Liability audits

Liability audits have really taken off in the UK. They are being commissioned by banks, insurance companies, lending institutions and by the clients themselves.

Often liability audits are referred to as *pre-acquisition audits*, where somebody is seeking to purchase a site or a company. They are useful in giving a company a good environmental bill of health before it is put up for sale. They can also be used prior to corporate mergers between companies. Purchasers want to ensure before they contemplate a merger that they are not buying environmental liabilities and problems of potential liabilities.

c) Waste minimisation audits

This type of audit has been carried out in the UK for the last 20 or 30 years. Any good product line manager will know about waste minimisation as failure to get it right will affect the bottom line.

Points to consider are:

- How the wastes are created.
- How they are managed.
- How they are disposed of.

Waste should be going to a regulated and licensed site. Contractors coming on to and off site with wastes should also be properly licensed and regulated. Management should be aware of the waste streams they produce and deal with those in a sensible and cost effective fashion. A company need not send all its waste from one site to 15 different waste contractors. This can be rationalised, perhaps using two or three contractors, and ensuring that the right specialists are chosen. Companies should ensure they have properly qualified people involved in waste management.

Waste minimisation seeks to reduce all types of waste through reduction at source and reuse or reprocessing. Reducing the amount of waste at source can be done by changing the process so that fewer raw materials are used.

Less wastage can be achieved by reviewing management systems. Where there is a poor and inefficient management system, increased waste disposal costs can result.

Reuse and recycling of wastes should be considered wherever possible so that some value can be built back into the company, with some costs reclaimed, instead of just paying out for disposal.

Components of an audit

Reviewing the scope

The main components of an audit are summarised in *diagram 8*. From the beginning when the scope of the audit is being reviewed management commitment is crucial. Once commitment has been secured it is necessary to decide on the scope of the audit, which means asking the following questions:

- What type of audit?

- Who will be involved?

- How will it be carried out?

- How much management time will be taken up during the audit?

- Who should the auditor see?

Diagram 8

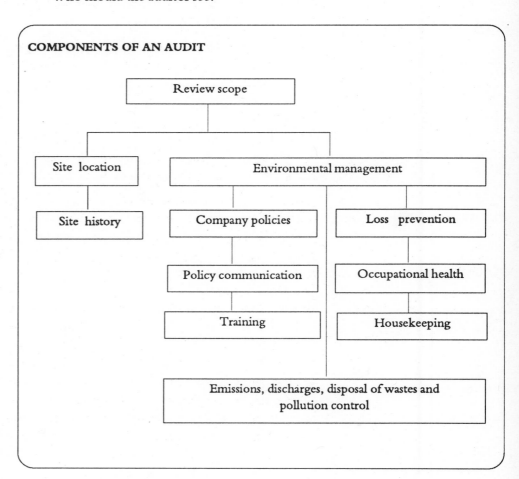

COMPONENTS OF AN AUDIT

- Who should be interviewed?

- What documentation will the auditor need to see?

Site location

During an audit the site location needs to be analysed in detail. In particular it is necessary to examine the geology, the hydrology, the hydro-geology, the soils and the vegetation if the site has large landholdings. The management of the site in the context of the community also needs to be examined.

Questions which need to be asked here include:

- Where is the site?

- Who are its neighbours?

- Who could be affected by the site?

- Are there old people's homes, or recreation grounds for children immediately adjacent to the site?

- Are there water courses that could be susceptible to pollution, or underground water supplies that are used for drinking water?

Site history

Researching the site history is critical to determine whether the land could be contaminated. This usually involves working through the planning records for the site, available at local libraries and Public Record Offices.

It is useful to talk to companies who previously occupied the site, to find out what processes they were involved in, how they disposed of their wastes, whether there was an enforcement history with respect to a particular site. It is worth finding out whether the old Alkali Inspectorate had dealings with the site. If so that would have a potential impact on the future running of that site, as the authorities could identify problems with contaminated land and request remediation.

Environmental management systems

With the introduction of BS 7750 companies need to look more closely at their environmental management systems. A useful way to do this is to analyse individually, key management areas such as policy, health and safety, and emissions/discharges, see *diagram 8*. (These divisions are purely arbitrary, as they can cross over quite readily into other areas, such as health, safety and occupational hygiene.)

a) Policy

Companies need to examine their existing environmental management systems, consider whether there is a company policy and how that policy is communicated at all levels within the company.

Policy communication is important. It is not sufficient for the board of directors to enthuse about an environmental policy, if the operatives on the lathes are tipping their cutting oils down the drains. The system must be followed through.

When the environmental management system is being evaluated, **training** must be considered. The amount spent and resources allocated on training should be examined. Are line managers and operators sent on training courses about the activities which cause environmental problems to the company? This can be a major problem with a lot of small and medium sized companies, because they are not actually training people.

Another point about training is that once the initial review of policy has been done, it may be desirable to re-audit. A company may wish to use in-house people, rather than expensive consultants. Companies should consider how to bring their people into the auditing process, letting them train alongside the professionals coming on site to do the actual audit.

b) Health and safety

Another key environmental management area to be studied is health, safety, and loss prevention.

Loss prevention covers how a company stores its products and wastes. How for example does a company ship and transport products round its site? Does it use tankers, drums, fork-lift trucks, or pipes? How do these actual transportation systems impact on the environment?

Occupational health may seem a strange thing to find in an environmental audit, but it is quite relevant. In the UK, but more so in the States, a lot of companies are facing litigation because of environmental problems causing asbestosis or other industrial diseases.

During the audit, the health records of employees should be examined. Is there a possibility that, prior to the company (now being audited) being on site there was a factory there regularly handling asbestos? Would some of those employees have transferred to the new company? Is there potentially any liability for litigation against the new company because of asbestos problems created in the past, where there was a transfer of the site or corporate assets?

An audit should consider house keeping. Often the first indication that the management systems on a particular site are not working is an untidy site with empty drums rolling around, pallets stored up against the doors and abandoned corners containing old products and wastes. If the manager is not getting around the site and doing a weekly housekeeping inspection he is not likely to be able to keep on top of a proper environmental management system.

c) Emissions/discharges

Questions which need to be asked when looking at the operational side of the company include the following:

- What sort of emissions are being discharged from chimney stacks and as fugitive emissions from workshops?

- How are these being dealt with?

- Is there compliance with the legislation?

- Is there a good relationship with the HMIP or with the local authorities?

Discharges could be contaminating the local town sewers as foul effluent. There could be surface water run off from the site going into surrounding ditches. The disposal of wastes, is a large component of the whole management of the site. This needs to be examined, as well as seeing how the company has geared itself up to dealing with wastes and controlling them on site. Waste should be stored safely and disposed of correctly into the appropriate types of sites and disposal facilities.

Contaminated land

Some legislation on contaminated land now on the statute books will come into force shortly and will relate to environmental auditing.

For further details on contaminated land legislation, see Chapter 4 on environmental legislation.

Contaminated land is:

> 'land containing substances be they liquids or solids when present in sufficent quantities or concentrations, can cause harm directly or indirectly to man and the environment' (*International Chamber of Commerce*)

There are many causes of contaminated land including:

- Historic use.

- Operational causes.

- Storage and transport.

- Leaks and spillages.

- Static emissions (e.g. particulates or volatile emissions (VOCs)).

- Waste disposal.

- Premises alterations.

- Sewage sludge.

The site history includes who was on the site before the current occupants. Britain's industrial heritage stretches back to 1750, there could have been many previous tenants on a particular site, so obviously the potential for contamination from historic industrial processes is enormous. It is necessary to build up a good historical picture when evaluating the potential of contamination.

Environmental auditing differs from environmental health and safety auditing because the latter looks very specifically at the site, e.g. what is in the perimeter fence. Environmental auditing is broader, as was stated in the International Chamber of Commerce definition. It is the impact of all the processes, and all the management systems actually on the broader environment.

People involved in property transactions who are buying, investing or lending money to a company with the intention of building value into that site when they take it over may want to reconstruct, redesign, put new premises there, new workshops, new plants, and equipment. If alterations to the site involve unearthing the ground, diverting the existing drainage system on the site, or modifying plant equipment, that could change the environmental management systems and unearth potential contamination that nobody knew about.

Contaminated land can be found on sites with very large landholdings, which perhaps have tenant farms which have been involved in the long term deposition of sewage sludge. Sewage sludge can contain a large amount of heavy metals, as well as other organic compounds which accumulate in the environment. This problem is now being examined by the Ministry of Agriculture. Certain particularly badly polluted areas are being scheduled as having had a contaminated use because of the disposal of sewage.

Implications of contaminated land for owners

The main implications of contaminated land for owners are:

- Liability for clean-up by the owner.

- Liability for clean-up by the local authority, (with passing on of charges).

- Litigation against company directors.

- Effect on the valuation of land/company.

- Difficulty of disposal of land/company.

- Problems in obtaining insurance.

Under the new legislation there is liability for clean-up. Enforcement authorities may enter a site where there has been a pollution incident, or where long term pollution is becoming apparent from that site. The local authority or HMIP can request that the owner or the Board of Directors of the company clean it up.

If the owner cannot afford to clean-up or does not know how to, the local authorities have powers to come on to the site, or to employ a contractor to clean-up the site and to charge the owner, or the Board of Directors.

Where negligence is proven, there is the possibility of litigation, either against the company as the corporate animal, or against the directors individually.

There are potential effects on valuation: where the clean-up cost exceeds the value of the business a net asset can be turned into a liability.

There may be specific problems in disposing of sites. Property investors who buy sites and companies with a view to selling them on could find their property difficult to sell if contamination was discovered. The unknown cost of clean-up and remediation could dramatically affect the value of the property. In order to sell it might be necessary to demonstrate either that the site had been cleaned up or that the pollution and the potential contamination would not have a significant bearing on a potential future use.

Implications of contaminated land for purchasers

If a company is intending to purchase a site or another company, what are the implications in this context?

After April 1993 if everything goes to schedule, there will be a register of land that has been in contaminative use. It will be drawn up at District County and Borough Council levels, during 1992. The register will contain all those sites that local authorities think may have had a contaminative use taking place within their boundaries. That can be a historical use, or current contaminative use.

This means that when potential purchasers of a site instruct their solicitors to do a search, the solicitors will find out whether or not the site is on the contaminated land register. If it is, the solicitor can rightly ask questions on behalf of the client, such as:'What is the liability? How will it affect the business?'

The purchaser can undertake a number of actions to protect himself. First of all, a warranty can be requested, but no company is going to give the sort of blanket environmental warranty that a lot of people have been demanding over the last six months. Secondly, the potential purchaser can re-negotiate the deal, bearing in mind the potential clean-up costs.

A lot of clients faced with these problems decide to withdraw from the deal, to look for a clean asset somewhere else.

Implications of contaminated land for lenders

The banks, lending institutions and pensions funds can have personal liability and if they can get involved with a company found to be contaminated they can have impaired security. Because they are lending against an asset, if the value of that asset changes, their security changes and their collateral base within the company changes.

Lenders may have to seek warranties and indemnities which borrowers are not prepared to give. In the US many lending institutions who stepped in after a company had gone into liquidation or receivership, suddenly found the US Environmental Protection Agency telling them that where there was a contamination problem they were now liable for cleaning it up. There have been several major cases in the States, worth millions of dollars where banks have been liable for cleaning up individual sites.

Costs of contamination clean-up

The Department of the Environment has suggested that there may be as many as 50,000–100,000 sites classified as contaminated. 40% of existing industrial sites in the UK will probably be registered. Removal of a cubic metre of contaminated soil means a cost of between £10 and a £100, so removing to a depth of one metre over an acre can cost between a £100,000 and £1 million. What's more, some contamination does not stop at a metre but goes down to 3 – 4 – 5 metres.

There is another case for special pollutants, such as PCB's, (Polychlorinated biphenyl). This is a very long-lived, toxic, carcinogenic organic compound. It hangs around the environment, does not degrade, and can be traced in minute quantities. Special pollutants need to be taken to one of two or three sites in the UK for disposal in high temperature rotary kiln incinerators. The cost of disposal is currently £1,800 per ton.

Key environmental legislation on contamination

For a full discussion of environmental legislation *see* Chapter 4.

Environmental Protection Act, Section 143

The Act covers registers of contaminated land, and will include present and previous contaminative use. Once registered, a company will not be able to take the site off the register even if it gets cleaned up.

The register is going to be a public record, so that anybody can actually look at the pollution, or potential pollution record of a site. It will be possible to look at the registration, what contamination is thought to be there, and then actually bring that out against a company in a public form.

Water Resources Act, Section 161

The Water Act 1989 was repealed on 1 December 1991, and replaced by the Water Resources Act 1991. There is a similar situation with Water, Section 115. Under that section of the Act, the National Rivers Authority is mandated to clean up pollution of rivers and other water courses or below ground water, such as aquifers. They can recover the cost from the polluter just like the local authorities or HMIP can and they have powers to stop polluting discharges.

Environmental Protection Act, Section 61

Section 61 in the Environmental Protection Act gives the same powers to the local authorities. They can inspect land and determine whether there is pollution emanating from previous contamination. They can enter on to that site and request it to be cleaned up. If the owner doesn't clean it, they can bring in their own contractors to do it and they can recover the cost from the owner or through the courts.

Benefits of environmental audits

If a company can demonstrate that its site is virtually contamination free because it has good environmental management systems, then potentially it could reduce its insurance premiums. For environmental impairment liability insurance policies all insurance companies demand that an environmental review or audit is undertaken.

It is possible to ensure that a company or site is complying with its own internal corporate policy or with legislation. A company can also seek to reduce its liabilities from potential litigation by individuals, by organisations, by local authorities and regulatory authorities.

Information from audits and reviews can be used to assist in emergency planning for a site, as well as into contingency planning systems.

There is no point in doing any environmental review or any environmental auditing unless the results are communicated, to the authorities to demonstrate competence, to clients and to suppliers, so they are all aware that the company is environmentally well organised and well managed. The results also need to be communicated within the company so staff have confidence in what the company is doing, and how it is managing its own shop. The public also need to be informed to give them confidence that the company is being properly managed.

The benefits are summarised in *diagram 9*.

Diagram 9

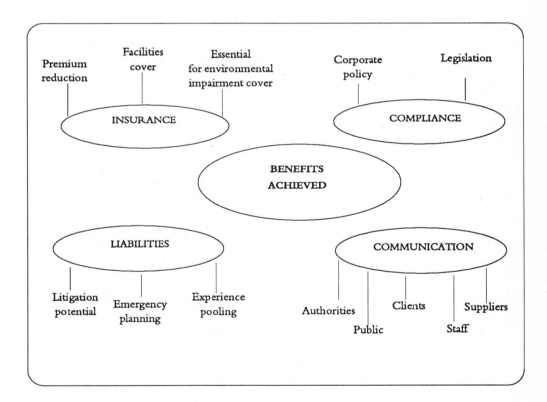

How to choose an environmental auditor

Choosing an environmental auditor can be difficult. How can you actually find an auditor, someone who has the confidence to do the sort of audit that you want? And, importantly, how do you fit that into the situation of your own establishment, whether it's a local authority, an industrial company or a company selling or manufacturing a product?

Firstly, you can decide whether or not to use external consultants. External consultants can be brought on to the site, they can set up a management system if one doesn't already exist, they can help to write or review an environmental policy, or design an implementation plan for that policy. The plan can be based on the company and its structure to produce an auditing programme that will work for that company.

A lot of companies are very short of resources, particularly human resources. They may not have people specifically trained in environmental auditing, and may need consultancy help. But it can be very valuable for companies to involve their staff at all stages in the auditing process.

A company wanting greater staff involvement might say to its consultants

> 'We want to do auditing, but we want to build the experience that we have within our company about our sites into the auditing system, so would you come and show us what sort of auditing programme we need? Can we discuss that and define it, and then build our own employees into this? Can we actually put those into the teams themselves so that operations managers, engineers, applied chemists, people that are operating on the sites, can actually gain from the whole exercise of auditing, so they get an overview what's involved in terms of environmental review?'

In those instances, once the auditing programme has been designed, two or three audits can be run at key sites that actually demonstrate how the audits will work. Then for succeeding audits, the auditors will use the company's own employees and put their lead auditors in. There is no point in doing an audit unless it is to be done periodically and reviewed in one, two or three years depending on the type of facility and the type of company.

But how can you guarantee that you choose the right consultants? There are various bodies that represent consultancy companies in the UK which they are seeking to lay down codes of practice, one such body is the Institute of Environmental Assessment (IEA).

The Institute of Environmental Assessment (IEA)

The IEA is a non profit making organisation, which is involved with the Government and the environmental consultancies. It has a registration board, and a system for self-certification. The IEA looks at the academic qualifications needed for individual membership, as well as membership of institutes, training and practical experience. There are three types of member.

- Trainee auditor.

- Environmental auditor.

- Lead auditor.

Questions

Question 1

Has the Institute of Environmental Assessment sensed any need to change its name, to reflect the 'auditing' aspect?

Answer

The IEA was originally formed to review the assessment of development type projects that would affect the environment, based on the Environmental Impact Assessment Directive. Environmental audits have increased greatly over the last two years. Consultancies who had started out working on planning and environmental impact assessement moved over to environmental auditing. The IEA was pushed by its members to move in the same direction.

Question 1 (cont.)

Did I understand you to say that a factory can obtain an eco-label?

Answer

Yes, this will be possible in the future. The Eco–Audit Directive involves using the eco-label in the eco-audit procedure. Any company which carries out an audit and makes the results publicly available can use an eco-label, but this will be site specific.

Question 2

In the US experience, consultants can be sued for what they did during the audit work. Are there any protective measures against this?

Answer

This is one of the reasons why the IEA originally moved to cover environmental auditing. An employer must have faith in the due diligence of the consultant. A consultant should secure an adequate level of professional indemnity. The employing company should question a consultancy on its cover, and write this into the proposal.

Question 3

How will local authorities go about compiling the contaminated land registers? Is the registration process contestible?

Answer

At present there is confusion on this in the UK. The local authorities seem to vary a lot on what procedure they will use. Some have made no decision yet, others are very specific, e.g. anything that was once a landfill site would go straight on the register.

Question 4

How far back will the local authorities look at the site history, when compiling the contaminated land registers? Will they use hearsay evidence?

Answer

At present the draft offers no right of appeal, except for erroneous entry.

6 What the auditor needs to know

Ted Allett, Environmental Resources Ltd, 106 Gloucester Place, London, W1H 3ZDB. Tel: 071-465 7278

Ted Allett is a lead auditor at Environmental Resources Ltd., the largest environmental consultancy in Britain. He is experienced in carrying out environmental audits in a number of fields, and is therefore well placed to discuss what the auditor needs to consider during the assessment.

This chapter covers the following:

- Liability audits.

- Technical audits.

- Management audits.

- Local authority audits.

- Quality assurance.

Introduction

This chapter looks at environmental auditing from the auditor's point of view, and includes examples of the practical problems experienced in carrying out audits.

Whatever type of audit is carried out the process before, during and after remains largely the same, as summarised in the following diagram.

Diagram 10

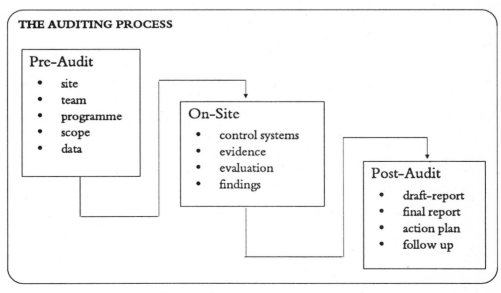

The term 'environmental auditing' was first used in the United States, for companies wanting to quantify their environmental risks, in a monetary sense, for a site purchase.

A problem for both clients and consultants is confusion over the type of audit that the client wants. Care must be taken to specify the scope of the audit and to be clear exactly why it is being carried out. Consultants need to sit down with their clients and distill from them their needs and any special requirements so that they can design the most appropriate audit. In this way the auditor can discover what type of business is involved and if there are any special issues which need to be taken into account. This may only take a couple of hours, but if it is not done, a lot of time and money can be wasted.

There are various ways of defining an audit, including the following types:

Liability audits

A liability audit is used to assess the environmental liabilities, usually prior to the acquisition or divestiture of a site, or a business. The client would be concerned about inheriting or buying an environmental liability, which would modify the value of the investment.

Diagram 11

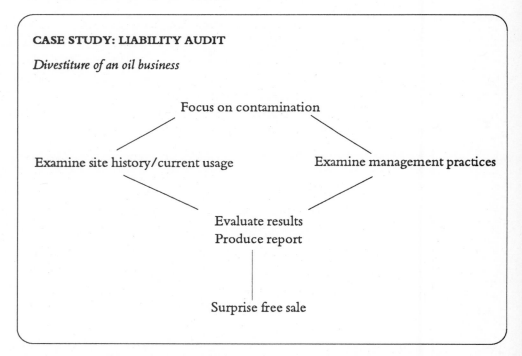

CASE STUDY: LIABILITY AUDIT

Divestiture of an oil business

Focus on contamination

Examine site history/current usage   Examine management practices

Evaluate results
Produce report

Surprise free sale

Diagram 11 shows how a liability audit on the divestiture of an oil business could be carried out. The focus would be on contamination, such as the cost of clearing up any ground contamination. The auditor would look at site history and current usage, for example the impact of spillage on the ground, and on water resources. The better the management practices in place, the less likelihood of ground contamination, so these practices would need to be examined as well.

The results would then be evaluated by the auditor, who would present the client with a report, which should enable the client to achieve a sale. It is somewhat like commissioning a survey before buying or selling a house. Auditors can be commissioned by either party involved in the sale.

A liability audit looks at management structure, as well as air, water and land pollution, waste disposal, materials handling and storage and contingency plans to deal with incidents.

When walking around a site, the auditor needs to look for evidence of previous building works, and to consider what their use was. It is not easy to get a history of the site, the auditor needs to look through land registry records, following previous ownership, and trying to establish what the site was previously used for. This will help to determine probability of contamination and would typically be carried out before any scientific examinations.

Spillage, stainage or an untidy appearance at a site will be cause for worry, and will show that the company is not being controlled with an eye to the possible risks. The auditor will check the site for examples of bad practice such as unlabelled tanks or drums, and will need to know whether the company uses hazardous chemicals or substances, such as poly-chlorinated biphenyls (PCB's) or asbestos and how they are handled..

One of the problems with liability audits occurs when the client does not yet own the site. The site manager may know that the auditor is visiting the site because of a takeover bid, but might be the only person on site who does. In this case, the best the auditor can hope for is the minimum of cooperation, with guided access to the site. Auditors have been asked to do acquisition audits without access to the site and are asked to go and look at the site from its public perimeters.

Auditors can suffer from extremely tight schedules for evaluating the situation and writing reports, because their work tends to be called for at the last minute, when the client is very close to signing a contract. Confidentiality can be a problem, where a name cannot be given.

Auditors would not expect to receive documentary evidence about the site. Clients, for example may have 'lost' their planning permission documents. This illustrates the difference in attitudes between acquisition audits and compliance, technical or management audits.

Technical audits

Diagram 12

> **CASE STUDY: TECHNICAL AUDITS**
>
> *Medium sized chemical company*
>
> • Examine compliance with legislation.
>
> • Examine compliance with company standards.
>
> • Internal liability assessment.
>
> • Evaluate results, produce audit report.
>
> → Action Programmes.

Technical and management audits are carried out as a management tool to help solve any problems. Primarily an in-house exercise, many companies use consultants to introduce an independent consistency check or to train or supplement in-house staff. With a technical audit, a company can look at its rate of compliance with environmental legislation, or with its own standards. A management audit looks at the management systems that are in place for controlling the management risks, so that compliance is achieved. Both technical and management staff therefore get involved in these types of audit. Auditors receive many commissions which are a blend of the two types.

Diagram 13

> **SCOPE OF TECHNICAL AUDITS**
>
> *Technical audits may consider:*
>
> • Site history.
>
> • Processes and materials used.
>
> • Emissions to air.
>
> • Discharges to water.
>
> • Spillage or disposal to ground.
>
> • Waste streams.
>
> • Permits and licences.

Technical audits in the United States are made more difficult, because there is so much environmental legislation to deal with. The auditor's job is made easier with access to the right knowlege and suitable databases. Auditors in America often take computers on to the site, and have developed prompting schemes, where the legislation is there as back up the questions being asked.

In the UK, the approach is somewhat different. There are few pieces of legislation which make it clear whether or not there is compliance. Much is a matter of interpretation. UK legislation, such as conditions for planning, discharge consent and emissions from chimneys are set on a local basis. The auditor needs to know about the framework legislation and to refer to the specific conditions attached to each site or process.

The purpose is to measure the environmental performance, and then to develop an action plan to put things right. The emphasis is more on emissions to air, discharges to water and the permits and licences involved.

While carrying out the audit of the site, it helps to be able to gain access to the highest point, to be able look down on the roofs of the buildings to identify and observe both controlled and unofficial emission sources.

Auditors need to have a ruthless eye, and still examine a site carefully, even if the first impression is that the site is particularly well organised.

Management Audits

Diagram 14

> **CASE STUDY: MANAGEMENT AUDITS**
>
> *Medium manufacturing company*
>
> • Examine existing responsibilities.
>
> • Review activities.
>
> • Consider actual and proposed legislation.
>
> • Examine the position of stakeholders.
>
> → Develop management structures and implement policy.

A management audit looks at systems for monitoring and for reporting up the organisational chain. It will examine whether there is an organisational chain which people understand and can use to communicate. If the procedures are in place, the company can be more confident that they are in control of their risks, and can produce environmental reports for their Board or the public.

Diagram 15

> **SCOPE OF MANAGEMENT AUDITS**
>
> • Policies, guidelines, etc.
>
> • Responsibilities.
>
> • Monitoring.
>
> • Purchasing.
>
> • Disposal.
>
> • Contingency plans.
>
> • Communications.

If the company has an environmental policy, the audit may consider whether it has moved on to produce a manual which explains what staff have to do, and details what their responsibilities are, contingency plans and communication chains?

With a management audit, the process can differ according to how deeply the auditor goes into the documentation. The headquarters client may not wish to burden the plant manager with the task of hunting out all the printed procedures, but it is not possible to state in a report that documentation exists, if the auditors have not seen it.

In the draft Eco-Audit Regulation, there is a verification stage, whereby a registered verifier looks again at the audit process and at the documentation for the management system. Quality assurance auditors have estimated that verification could take up to five times as long as the original management audit did. The client will not want to pay for this. Now it is thought that the final version of the Eco-Audit Regulation will play down the verification stage and just look at the final statements, rather than all the processes leading up to them.

Local authority audits

Local authority audits grew up as a result of the Friends of the Earth Charter. The Local Government Management Board has now produced a guide to help people decide whether or not to do an audit in-house, and which type to use. A local authority audit is like a technical audit, but on a grand scale. It can involve an enormous amount of data, but the local authority should be able to collate that itself, and then get the auditor to review it. Review of policies is perhaps better done by an external auditor, who can bring a more detatched eye to the foundation stones of the authority.

Local authorities are moving towards the BS 7750 way of working. The Department of the Environment have commissioned research into whether local authorities could directly apply BS 7750 or the Eco-Audit Regulation or whether they would need modification.

Quality assurance

There are a number of quality criteria which can be applied to auditing.

- Objectivity.

- Competence of the team.

- Methodology.

- Replicability.

- Benefits.

Perhaps the most difficult to achieve of these is replicability. Two audit teams should find the same set of recommendations. This is more likely to happen in the United States, than in Britain, because of our interpretive environmental legislation. Audits in Britain are done by interpretation against good practice, which is determined by the auditor's experience. Replicable audits are therefore more difficult to achieve in the UK context. A number of initiatives are underway, to address some of the issues raised by these criteria, including Codes of Practice by the Association of

Environmental Consultancies and the Institute of Environmental Assessment.

Questions

Question 1

What are the really essential things to be confident about when undertaking the scoping exercise?

Answer

Is it a liability or compliance audit? With a company audit this means looking at the organisation's own management practices, there may or may not be a policy in place. If there is none, the company needs to look around its site, comparing what is found with the legislation, looking at the various stakeholders, the employees, consumers, investors in the business, and identifying the environmental risks and how the company is responding to them.

The company should try and identify exactly what its policy should address. A lot of company policies are very general and do not reflect the business that the company is in. Once a company has a policy, the audit is geared by its objectives, to tell the company whether it is achieving them. If it is a highly complex manaufacturing process, the auditor is looking closely at all pollution streams and waste management. If it is a retail company, they are much more concerned with the product and marketing end, for example, false advertising claims.

Question 2

Should the policies of all manufacturing companies look the same?

Answer

There are many diverse businesses that have essentially the same short statement of policy.

If the policy does not address the particular problems of the business, then arguably it is not a very helpful policy. It does not, for example, help the auditor sort out the environmental priorities of the company. Ten sentence policies are not unusual; but this could easily be doubled. The policy should state why the company is in business, and what the specific environmental effects of the business are.

Question 3

How do you chose the auditing team? How can quality assurance be guaranteed?

Answer

The auditor should build a team based on what the client has told them about the business. They will take a person who has experience of that type of industry.

Team leaders usually have a basic engineering or scientific discipline, and a maturity to deal with the human element of an audit, where the auditor has to achieve a considerable degree of cooperation. The auditor might have to deal with a site manager who has had the audit forced on him. The process does not always begin with an easy relationship.

Maturity and experience in a team leader are vital. It is good to have someone who has had experience working in a business organisation, and who has been on ten or twenty audits already (in the case of a leader). Larger consultancies can bring people on as they can give them much broader experience.

A corporate audit can often include a review of strategic issues for the company, which the Board would be concerned with. It will include some visits to sites to weigh up the environmental risk and management systems, as well as product audits.

7 Reaping the benefits

Krystyna Krajewska and Paul Ingrams, Greenmantle, Thornbury House, 18 High Street, Cheltenham, Gloucestershire, GL50 1DZ. Tel: 0242 255387

Krystyna Krajewska and Paul Ingrams are founder Directors of Greenmantle – the business communications consultancy with a particular focus on social and environmental issues in business and the fundraising voluntary sector. They have experience in helping companies to make the most of their environmental audits, by ensuring proper follow-up after the original audit and by publicising the results of the audit to the right groups.

This chapter looks at environmental auditing in a broader business context, topics covered include:

- Environmental auditing – master or servant?

- Environmental policy.

- The opportunities and benefits.

- Public and stakeholder access to information.

- 'Green messages' (the mistakes that companies are making at the moment in marketing a green image.)

Environmental auditing – master or servant?

As the following table shows, there has been a phenomenal growth of environmental consultancies over the last couple of years.

Diagram 16

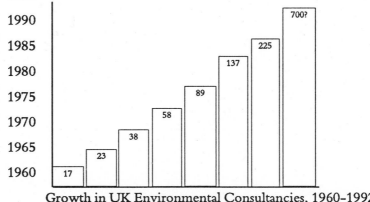

Growth in UK Environmental Consultancies, 1960–1992
(Source: *ENDS Directory* 1992)

51

The work of environmental auditors can be broken down into a number of key areas. The following diagram gives a breakdown of the main areas of work. Environmental impact assessment, the most popular area of work, covers the monitoring of facts and figures, and this is what influences people the most.

Diagram 17

MAIN AREAS OF ENVIRONMENTAL CONSULTANCY (% OF 1991 LIST):

Environmental impact assessment	14.8
Water pollution	13.0
Waste management	12.1
Contaminated land	10.5
Air pollution, etc.	8.1
Corporate environmental strategy	4.6

(Source: *ENDS Directory* 1991)

The area that takes up the smallest amount of auditor's work is the development of corporate environmental strategies. The reason may be that companies are assuming that all environmental policies are already sorted out, or that it doesn't matter. In fact this is a crucial area for companies to consider.

If there are still doubts that environmental auditing is here to stay, *diagrams 16* and *17* prove otherwise. There is now pressure on industry to avoid prosecution and to comply with new legislation and there is also a move to introduce environmental credits and taxes. The benefits of environmental auditing go beyond simply avoiding prosecution, to making sure that a business can be insured or financed in future, and that a company can carry on trading.

But there are a number of dangers inherent in environmental auditing, and these fall into three areas.

- A company which has paid a lot of money for an audit feels that it has done its bit for the environment and can maybe sit on its laurels.

- When a professional comes into a business and approves its activities, there is the danger that the company might think it is doing everything it needs to.

- By reducing environmental performance to raw data there is a danger that companies may forget why performance needs to be monitored and why processes need to be controlled in the first place.

It should not be forgotten that environmental auditing has come about because there is growing pressure outside business to look after our planet and to leave some sort of world for our grandchildren. That is the real motivating factor.

> 'We are in danger of getting things the wrong way round. You cannot start with an audit, neither can you manage on the basis of an audit – you must start with a Policy.'
> *(Ian Brice, senior Environmental Manager at Shell Petroleum).*

Environmental policy A policy is more than a statement of good intentions. Indeed, it is more than the development of codes of practice or operational guidelines. It is a set of measures intended to work together to achieve a specific goal, in this case the improvement of the environment. It seems that quite a large number of companies have an environmental policy. But it often consists of a nicely produced brochure which is used to say proudly; 'This is what we are doing, our PR people have printed this.'

Once a corporate policy is based on environmental auditing, then the facts and figures produced by the audit process allow a company to proceed beyond the mere waving of the booklet, towards the incorporation of a policy which will enable them to get on with all their neighbours.

A basic question that needs to be asked is – what is the environment? There is not really any satisfactory working definition at the moment. Is it simply the working environment, bounded by the factory walls? Or is it the area around the workplace, where the company has the most immediate impacts? Indeed, it could be the entire world, and there are many people who are putting pressure on business to take responsibility for improving the world as a whole.

Business people may not be ready for this yet, but it is coming. Within ten years there could be a system for licensing all production on the basis of social need.

Company environmental policy should define the corporate response to environmental issues. Environmental policy underlines corporate commitment for meeting the relevant legal requirements. The policy defines an action plan for meeting or exceeding those requirements, and companies which go beyond the letter of the law tend to be defined as 'leading edge', that is they gain a significant market advantage by doing so.

An environmental policy also introduces a timetable for action, although that timetable is increasingly being imposed from outside by various EC Directives, some of which have been taken up and some of which haven't. Whatever one thinks of the individual Directives we have to live with them, and if we look for the opportunities rather than just the pressures, then we can make progress.

The essential ingredients of an environmental policy are as follows:

- There should be a published statement.

- There should be clear objectives, so that a company can motivate management behind it, and importantly, give the workforce a sense of ownership of the policy.

- A Board member should be appointed with environmental responsibility, as the CBI Environment Business Forum membership rules insist.

- It is clear that policy has to be set at the top, and owned at the bottom. In the middle, management is squeezed from both directions. As middle management will be in charge of implementing environmental policy it is crucial that they are included in the policy making procedures to ensure their commitment and ability to implement the standards required.

- A clear Communications Plan is very important, otherwise things can go awry, as for instance when BP at Immingham released a large and, as it happened, quite harmless purple cloud which floated alarmingly over the residents of Hull. Within two hours the switchboard was jammed, so that they could not telephone out to the managers who needed to be brought in to manage the problem. Crisis management is where the communication plan starts, but where it seems to finish these days is with having to withdraw expensive advertising campaign because environmental claims have been made that do not stand up to public scrutiny. In this sort of situation business communications experts such as Greenmantle can help by being communicators first, and environmentalists second.

- Staff need to be made aware of company environmental policy and fully trained to handle their new responsibilities. Without consideration of training needs an environmental policy cannot work. At the moment the relevant standards covering training are British Standard BS 5750 on quality management and the environmental performance standard BS 7750.

- At present there are a number of environmental training and educational institutions offering qualifications (there is now even an Environmental MBA at Manchester University).
  In America, management trainees graduating with an environmental qualification are attracting salary premiums of 30%. The increasing availability of formal training courses in this area has resulted partly from the growth of environmental auditing.

- Finally, the policy must include the environmental and health and safety checks which are ongoing in most companies anyway.

Diagram 18 shows the Policy Trail, how a policy is formulated and what happens to it when it begins to be implemented.

Diagram 18

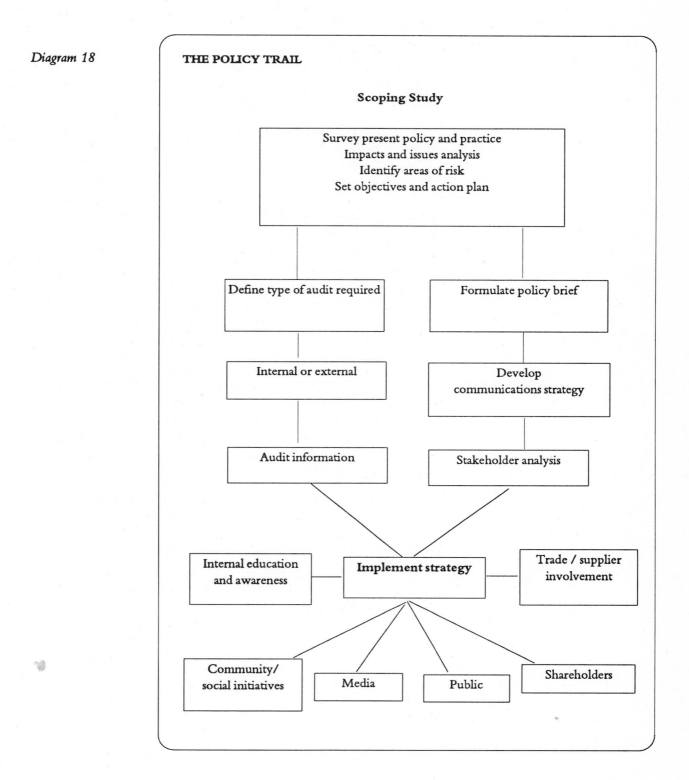

THE POLICY TRAIL

Scoping Study

Survey present policy and practice
Impacts and issues analysis
Identify areas of risk
Set objectives and action plan

Define type of audit required

Formulate policy brief

Internal or external

Develop communications strategy

Audit information

Stakeholder analysis

Internal education and awareness

Implement strategy

Trade / supplier involvement

Community/ social initiatives

Media

Public

Shareholders

The policy making process starts with a scoping study to identify the areas needing consideration. The left hand channel shows the technical side, defining the type of audit required – what's being done well, and what is not being done so well. On the right is the need to formulate a policy brief and to develop the communication plan. Both those channels then impact on the 'Implement strategy' box

Implementing strategy involves raising internal awareness to get both the management and workforce in support. It also means talking to outside buyers and suppliers to obtain their cooperation.

After considering suppliers companies should then go on to examine community and social issues – this is where they could spend a little more of their advertising budget on environmental Good Neighbour projects, instead of spending it on TV, telling everybody how green they are.

Finally, of course, there are the media and other stakeholders – shareholders, city investors, customers, and so on, to whom a company needs to communicate in a targeted and responsive way.

As a final word of warning, when producing an environmental policy companies should ensure that the policy accurately reflects either where a business is, or where it is hoping to get to, otherwise they will surely be found out!

Opportunities and benefits

The previous Environment Secretary, Michael Heseltine, talked a lot about the opportunities within Europe. There is a £2,000 billion market in Europe and America. That market is there for the consultants in the field, but also for companies that have the vision and imagination to grasp the opportunities. Businesses should look carefully when they audit, there will be a lot of information created, and this may be used to tap into new markets.

Regarding the rise of the 'green consumer', it has been said that it will no longer be enough simply to make a few changes to products, label them as green, charge a premium and then sit back and watch the money roll in. The 'green consumer' is becoming wiser and more sophisticated and is taking wider issues, such as ethical marketing, into consideration.

Michael Heseltine also commented that, 'Business success and environmental success are nearly always found in association with each other.' Small and medium sized companies often argue that they simply cannot afford to take the environment on board. Yes, it is expensive, but the opportunities are also there to identify new markets, new products, and to switch to more efficient methods of operating. That has got to be the way forward.

To summarise the benefits, many of the companies that are aware of the environment and aware of their consumers are developing new products. There are new niche markets to be found in which to diversify. The company's experience of environmental auditing can be offered to others as a consultancy. If a firm has undergone an audit, they have gone through quite an expensive learning curve, and this can be recouped by passing on their experience, it is all valuable information for others. A company can gain status by being responsible, providing benefits to the industry, its employees and the community.

It may take years, and will not be easy. Many pressure groups are watching the development of environmentalism in business with a keen eye, as they are ready to trip up people who don't meet their impeccable standards.

Public access to information

In January 1992 the *ENDS Report* commented:

> 'Over the next few years, public access to information on environmental performance will be extended considerably by law... but momentum to wider disclosure is also coming from a number of voluntary initiatives.'

Information is the key to developing a more environmentally aware approach, and there is a lot of pressure for full disclosure, and for companies to be franker about their activities. Every company that carries out an audit is producing more and more data, and somebody has to actually extract that information, decide what is valuable and translate it to the different stakeholders, making it sensible and effective for the company in marketing terms.

Stakeholder analysis

Throughout the policy making and implementation process companies need to consider who the policy is going to influence. *Diagram 19* shows a number of groups companies might seek to influence, and who might influence the company.

Diagram 19

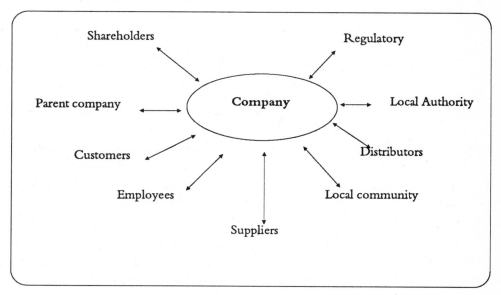

At the planning stage it is necessary to consider the many and various information channels and how each of these different groups perceive the company. The analysis will show where the communications are poor, where they don't even exist – or where they are strong enough to build on.

What happens after the policy is formulated is in many ways a simple marketing exercise. A business needs to see how their environmental policy tracks through all the different communication tools that they use. They may have a sales force communicating regularly with customers and prospective customers, these staff need to be fully aware of what the policy is, how it affects their products and how they can communicate the benefits. All the usual ways of reflecting brand strengths should reflect the commitment to environmental quality from telesales, marketing promotions, direct mail, corporate advertising, into press and public relations, recruitment and community initiatives.

Green messages

There are numerous examples of where companies have come unstuck through not leading on environmental communications policy, but instead leaving it to outside agencies.

For example the Advertising Standards Authority had to ask car manufacturer Peugeot Talbot to withdraw an advertisement for its diesel cars after it was not able to substantiate a claim that diesels were cleaner than petrol driven cars.

Now, obviously, it is very expensive to pull out of an advertising campaign at the last minute, and it is best to be sure of the ground at the beginning. We are seeing new disciplines emerging, such as Life Cycle Analysis, and new ways of looking at products and processes. It is tempting, but very dangerous – until the techniques become more sophisticated – to actually start using these as the basis of marketing claims.

Diagram 20

> **Summary**
> In summary, there are three simple points:
>
> * Do not do an audit without a policy! Be clear why it is being done and what will be done with the information obtained.
>
> * Plan the communication strategy carefully. Target stakeholders, be prepared to monitor developments and adapt accordingly.
>
> * Remember that there is only one certainty in environmental management which is that the issues will change from day to day!
>
> Scientific knowledge of the environment is being constantly updated. No matter how much effort is put into planning a policy, a company has to be prepared to change it just as quickly as their audit tells them they need to.

8 Sources of information on environmental auditing

Helen Woolston, The British Library, Environmental Information Service, 25 Southampton Buildings, London WC2A 1AW. Tel: 071-323 7955

Helen Woolston has spent two years working with the British Library's Environmental Information Service gaining experience of answering clients' enquiries and using printed and computerised sources. She has an interest in sources of environmental legislation, business issues such as audits, policies and recycling and science issues such as global warming. She is the co-author of the recently published book *Environmental information: a guide to sources*.

This chapter covers the following:

- Organisations.

- Environmental policy documents.

- Journals (including trade journals).

- Computerised databases.

- Catalogues.

- Hosts.

Introduction

Requests for information on environmental auditing usually fall into one of the following categories:

- Case studies.

- Environmental policies.

- How to carry out an audit.

- Who can carry out audits for you.

- How to choose an auditor.

Information on environmental auditing has always been high on the list of enquiry topics at the British Library's Environmental Information Service. Questions range from requests to know what it actually is, to those wanting the latest published papers on the subject. It is easy for a company which knows its way around the information sources to keep up to date with the latest developments in environmental auditing and its associated legislation.

There are several sources to look at when searching for auditing information, as summarised below.

- Organisations
- Conferences
  CBI
  Brunel University
- Journals
- Books
- Databases
- Legal material

Organisations

Often, if you know the right organisation to contact, the battle is almost won. The following list includes some of the organisations well known for their involvement in environmental auditing issues.

Association of Environmental Consultancies (AEC)
The Association has established a scheme for registering environmental auditing consultancies. The consultancy must agree to comply with the AEC Code of Practice, to supply information about its experiences, resources, training, and to have independent verification.

The Association has members from the UK and overseas. They can be associate or full members. Full members must have at least three senior staff with ten or more years experience, and employ at least ten consultants with an average of two years of experience, among other criteria.

Other functions include the provision of a forum for environmental consultancies to discuss important issues, and making available information on environmental consultancies.

Address: Priestley House, 28–34 Albert Street, Birmingham, B4 7UD
Tel: 021-616 1010

Association of Metropolitan Authorities
The Association is the professional body for the metropolitan authorities. It is involved in collating their response to environmental audits and reviews, and in advising members on how best to carry them out. They have published a number of advisory reports.

Address: 35 Great Smith Street, London SW1P 3BJ. Tel: 071-222 8100

British Standards Institution

The BSI published BS 7750 on environmental management systems in March 1992. Copies are available for sale from them, and they will give advice on implementing the standard.

Address: Linford Wood, Milton Keynes, MK4 6LE.
Tel: 0908 221166

Confederation of British Industry (CBI)

The Environment Management Unit at the CBI has been working for a long time to help members deal with environmental problems, and make the most of environmental opportunities. They produce *Environment News*, which comes out quarterly, and covers all the latest developments and initiatives.

Those who are not CBI members can still join the Environment Business Forum. Companies who join must have an environmental policy.

The CBI also coordinates responses from British Industry to EC initiatives.

Address: Centre Point, 103 New Oxford Street, London, WC1A 1DU.
Tel: 071-379 7400

Department of Trade and Industry

Various sections of the Department of Trade and Industry are closely involved in work with industry and environment. There is an Environment Management Unit, which gives advice and help to companies and coordinates UK responses to legislation, particularly the EC Eco-audit regulation proposals. They produce the Spearhead database, and a number of relevant publications. The *Guide to Contacts in Government Departments for the Environment* is a very useful collection of names and contact phone numbers, arranged by environmental subject. This is updated periodically, and is available free of charge.

Address: 123 Victoria Street, London SW1E 6RB. Tel: 071-215 1042

Environmental Data Services Ltd. (ENDS)

ENDS produces the *Directory of Environmental Consultants*, which was originally published in 1990, a third edition was published in 1992. The *Directory* was the first comprehensive listing of its kind, and includes a useful chapter on the markets for environmental consultancies. When using the *Directory* one should keep in mind that the consultants have written their own entries.

ENDS undertake research projects in the field of environmental auditing.

Address: Unit 24, Finsbury Business Centre, Bowling Green Lane, London EC1R 0NE. Tel: 071-278 4745

**European Communities Commission Information
Office/European Parliament Information Office**
It can be difficult to obtain copies of EC legislation, for example, the
Eco-Audit Regulation has only been available in various draft forms until
recently.

However, many central libraries are European Documentation Centres,
and collect EC legislation. Copies of Directives and Regulations can also
be obtained through HMSO.

The best way of gaining access to the legislation, as well as advice, is to
contact either the European Commission Information Office, or the
European Parliament Information Office. Each can advise on the progress
of legislation through either the Commission or Parliament, and both have
libraries which can be visited to see the legislation.

Address: European Communities Commission Information Office, 8
Storey's Gate, London SW1P 3AT. Tel: 071-973 1992

Address: European Parliament Information Office, 2 Queen Anne's Gate,
London SW1H 9AA. Tel: 071-222 0411.

Friends of the Earth (FoE)
This pressure group has produced the Local Authorities' Charter, and has
worked with a number of authorities on developing environmental audits.
FoE have also produced a briefing sheet *Environmental audits of local
authorities: terms of reference*.

Address: 26-28 Underwood Street, London N1 7JQ. Tel: 071-490 1555

Institute of Environmental Assessment
This is an independent, professional body for environmental consultants,
dedicated to the raising of environmental assessment standards. It produces
the largest UK database of environmental consultancies, in which it
independently assesses good quality work and includes qualifications, skills
and experience of individuals. The Institute also produces the largest UK
database on environmental statements, which contains detailed records. A
library of the statements is available for consultation.

The Institute aims to provide independent scientific advice to industry and
planning authorities on environmental matters, for example, producing a
project outline for the environmental statement. It is involved in
developing guidelines on best practice environmental techniques, and
produces a regular newsletter to inform members of new developments.

Consultancies first join the Institute as Associate Assessor members, but
their environmental statements are independently assessed, and they can
move up to Registered status.

Address: Holbeck Manor, Horncastle, Lincolnshire, LN9 6PU.
Tel: 0507 533444

London Research Centre (LRC)
Formed after the dissolution of the Greater London Council (GLC), this library and information centre runs the ACOMPLINE, URBALINE and RESLINE databases. They specialise in local authority and urban issues and hold a large stock of material on environmental auditing.

Address: Research Library, Parliament House, Black Prince Road, London SE1 7SZ. Tel: 071-735 4250

Trades Union Congress (TUC) and other Unions
The TUC has produced the useful booklet *Greening the Workplace*, which aims to help trade union members work for high standards of environmental performance and pollution control. It summarises important environmental issues, and provides a starting point for developing an environmental policy.

Many other individual trade unions are also actively involved in producing environmental policies, and educating their members as to what they can achieve at work. Details are available from the TUC, or the particular union.

Address: Congress House, Great Russell Street, London WC1B 3LS.
Tel: 071-636 4030

Environmental policy documents

Several companies find it useful to look at other company environmental policies as an aid, before they begin to work on their own. It is also beneficial to make the policy publicly available, so that the environmental achievements of the company can be assessed.

At the present time, several organisations are making a collection of company environmental policies. These include the Environment Council's Business and Environment Programme, who will also advise on writing a policy. The British Library's Environmental Information Service also has a collection of green policy documents, as do a number of consultancy companies.

Address: Environment Council, 80 York Way, London N1 9AG.
Tel: 071-278 4736

Journals

Environmental Management
This journal has now incorporated the closed title *Environmental Auditor* and therefore includes a high proportion of relevant coverage on auditing. It is an American magazine, and is published every two months.

Publisher: Springer Verlag, 175 Fifth Avenue, New York, NY 10010
USA, Tel: (212) 460 1500
Frequency: Bimonthly
ISSN 0364-152X

ENDS Report
From Environmental Data Services Ltd, the *ENDS Report* has been published since 1978 and has achieved an enviable reputation for providing details of new and proposed legislation very quickly. It regularly covers environmental auditing and the organisations involved. It includes conference details and a vacancies column.

Publisher: ENDS Ltd, Unit 24, Finsbury Business Centre, Bowling Green Lane, London. Tel: 071-278 4745
Frequency: Monthly
SRIS Classmark: Holborn(P) BY 25-E(25)

Environment Business
Environment Business is a loose-leaf publication, which aims to keep the businessman aware of important environmental issues. As well as the regular newsletter, there are often specific update inserts. There have been two inserts on industrial environmental auditing, the latest published in September 1991. These are excellent summaries of the subject, providing an introduction and guide to different types of audit and detailing the points which should be covered in an audit.

Publisher: Information for Industry Ltd, 521 Old York Road, London SW18 1TG. Tel: 081-877 9130
Frequency: Fortnightly
ISSN 0959-7042

Simmons and Simmons Environmental Law Newsletter/Denton Hall Burgin and Warrens Environmental Law Newsletter
These are two examples of very useful newsletters which are published by environmental law groups within solicitors' firms. These aim to update readers on the latest environmental legislation, including any on environmental auditing. They also often produce booklets which describe particular pieces of legislation in detail.

Publisher: Simmons and Simmons, 14 Dominion Street, London EC2M 2RJ. Tel: 071-628 2020
Frequency: Quarterly

Publisher: Denton Hall Burgin and Warrens, Cliffords Inn, 5 Chancery Lane, London. Tel: 071-242 1212
Frequency: Quarterly

Trade journals

Almost all sectors of industry and business have well established trade journals, which cover all the issues of importance to that trade. As environmental performance has become so important to all industry sectors, it is increasingly common to find specialised articles on how environmental auditing fits into a particular industry in its trade journal. It is practically a case of choosing the trade journal for the industry of interest, and scanning through its past issues.

Examples of trade journals which frequently cover environmental issues include:

Chemistry and Industry
Publisher: Society of Chemical Industry, 14 Belgrave Square, London
SW1X 8PS. Tel: 071-235 3681
Frequency: Monthly
ISSN 0009-3068
SRIS Classmark: Holborn (P) LT00-E(12)

Engineer
Publisher: Morgan-Grampian Ltd, Morgan-Grampian House, 30
Calderwood Street, London SE18 6QH. Tel: 081-855 7777
Frequency: Weekly
ISSN 0013-7758
SRIS Classmark: Holborn (P) SR00-E(41)

Planner
Publisher: Royal Town Planning Institute, 26 Portland Place, London
W1N 4BE. Tel: 071-636 9107
Frequency: 50/year
ISSN: 0309-1384
SRIS Classmark: Holborn (P) WF 00-E(2)

Surveyor
Publisher: Reed Business Publishing Ltd, Quadrant House, The Quadrant,
Sutton, Surrey SM2 5AS. Tel: 081-661 4661
Frequency: Weekly
ISSN: 0039-6303
SRIS Classmark: Holborn (P)VW35-E(2)

Water Bulletin
Publisher: Water Services Association of England and Wales, 1 Queen
Anne's Gate, London SW1H 9BH. Tel: 071-222 8111
Frequency: Weekly
ISSN: 0262-9909
SRIS Classmark: Holborn (P) SL324-E(2)

This is a limited list, as there are many more examples to be found.

Computerised databases

General/science

ACOMPLINE
This is produced by the London Research Centre, and lists their holdings. It is twinned with URBALINE, which covers newspaper articles. The subject coverage is local government, urban studies and management.
Host: ESA-IRS Dialtech
Tel: 071-323 7951

Chemical Abstracts (CA Search)
This database covers every possible aspect of chemistry, in 9 million records. It contains environmental auditing references of interest to the chemical industry.
Host: STN (the only host which has abstracts)

Chemical Business Newsbase (CBNB)
Produced by the Royal Society of Chemistry, this database covers business issues of interest to the chemical industry. There has been a big increase in the amount of material on environmental auditing and associated legislation on this database over the last three years.
Host: Dialog

ENVIROLINE
This is the online equivalent of *Environmental Abstracts*. It is produced by Bowker in the USA, and about 70% of its records are taken from American sources. ENVIROLINE is the largest database dealing specifically with the environment. There are approximately 160,000 references, from 1971 onwards. All environmental topics are covered, including pollution of air, water and land, but it does contain a significant amount of literature on environmental auditing. It is useful for pinpointing the American methods of auditing.
Hosts: Dialog, ESA-IRS Dialtech, Orbit
CD-ROM version: Enviro/Energyline Abstracts Plus

Environmental Bibliography
This database corresponds to the printed abstracting journal *Environmental Periodicals Bibliography*. It has a similar subject coverage to ENVIROLINE, but it uses a different list of sources, so there is not always overlap. The major drawback is that there are no abstracts of the records, simply bibliographic details and indexing.
Host: Dialog

Pollution Abstracts
The database is more specialist than ENVIROLINE in that it is particularly concerned with information on pollution. It does not cover conservation or wildlife in any detail. The database has a printed equivalent with the same name, and is produced by Cambridge Scientific Abstracts. It has a similar American bias to ENVIROLINE. There are records on Pollution

Abstracts about environmental auditing, mainly in the pollution control industries.
Hosts: Data-Star, Dialog, ESA-IRS Dialtech

Note: it is possible to search these three databases (ENVIROLINE, Environmental Bibliography and Pollution Abstracts) together as one database, on Dialog. Any duplicate records found can be removed.

Business

PTS PROMT
This is the online equivalent of the printed *Predicasts Overview of Markets and Technology*. It contains about 1.5 million citations, and takes its records from a very wide range of business sources. The database contains abstracts with selected full text and can be excellent for searching for issues such as green consumerism and eco-labelling, as well as environmental auditing itself.
Hosts: Data-Star, Dialog

PTS Newsletter Database
This contains the full text of about 500 newsletters, published worldwide (but with an American bias). The newsletters are concerned with strategic developments which affect business and industry. There are a number of relevant environmental titles, such as *Business in the Environment*, *Environment Business Journal*, and *Green Marketing Report*.
Hosts: Data-Star, Dialog

Stockbroker Investment Reports: DRT EC and Eastern Europe Business Database; Investext
DRT and Investext are examples of online databases which contain the full text of stockbroker reports. The stockbroker reports analyse the futures of particular business sectors, including the effects of particular events on a range of companies. Both these databases contain, amongst other material, valuable analysis of what the Eco-Audit Regulation will mean to British business.
Host: Data-Star

Textline
This is good for searching the media. It contains the full text of all the quality newspapers, as well as magazines such as the *Economist* and *New Scientist*. The amount of material on environmental auditing on this database has increased dramatically over the last two years, reflecting the quantity of information in the newspapers. There is a bias towards business issues, but the environment is fast becoming a business issue. Textline can be searched in a number of ways, including heading and first paragraph only. It is rather expensive to use, but not when compared with the resources needed to maintain a newspaper cuttings library.
Hosts: Data-Star, Dialog

Legislation

CELEX

This is produced by the EC and contains the full text of all legislation. It does not contain proposed legislation, only that which has been passed by the Parliament and Commission. The drawbacks of using CELEX include its poor indexing, and the fact that the appendices of the pieces of legislation, often containing the most pertinent information, are not usually available.
Host: Data-Star
CD-ROM version: JUSTIS

Spearhead

The database is produced by the Department of Trade and Industry and has no printed equivalent. It looks at issues involved in the 1992 single market. This includes environmental legislation, such as the Eco-Audit Regulation. Whilst it is not a full text database there are abstracts. One of Spearhead's main bonuses is that it contains proposed legislation, and it traces it through the various EC procedures. Another benefit is that each record contains a phone number for a DTI contact who can advise on the latest progress of the legislation.

It is useful to use Spearhead in conjunction with CELEX. Spearhead has more comprehensive indexing, making it easier to find material on the required topic, with associated document numbers. These numbers can be used in CELEX to find the full text of the documents.
Host: Data-Star
CD-ROM version: soon to be available for the DTI

Online Catalogues

System for Information on Grey Literature in Europe (SIGLE)

This is the online equivalent of *British Reports, Translations and Theses*. It is good for tracing reports, which are published informally, or not through the normal channels. Many items of an environmental interest can only be found in this way.
Host: BLAISE-LINE

DSC Monographs

From the British Library Document Supply Centre (DSC), this contains 544,000 citations (after 1980) of monographs at DSC. It is good for finding textbooks on environmental auditing. All items found in this catalogue can be borrowed from The British Library Document Supply Centre (DSC) using their inter-library loan scheme. Contact DSC on 0937 843434 for information on how to become a registered user.
Host: BLAISE-LINE

BNBMARC

This contains bibliographic information on all books and first issues of periodicals which have been published in Great Britain and deposited with

the British Library's Copyright Receipt Office since 1950. It is good for checking the latest titles on environmental auditing, as it often has records provided by publishers before the book is actually published.
Host: BLAISE-LINE

LCMARC: Books All
This contains bibliographic information on about 2.8 million monographs published worldwide since 1968. It contains titles of various languages, but is predominantly American. The database corresponds in part to the Library of Congress National Union Catalog.
Hosts: BLAISE-LINE, Dialog

Hosts

BLAISE-LINE
Boston Spa
Wetherby, West Yorkshire
LS23 7BQ
Tel: 0937 546585

Data-Star (Marketing) Ltd
5th Floor, Plaza Suite
114 Jermyn Street
London SW1Y 6HJ
Tel: 071-930 5503

Dialog Information
Retrieval Service
Woodside
Hinksey Hill
Oxford OX1 5AU
Tel: 0865 730275

ESA-IRS Dialtech
The British Library
Science Reference and Information
Service
25 Southampton Buildings
London WC2A 1AW
Tel: 071-323 7951

Orbit Search Service
Achilles House
Western Avenue
London W3 0UA
Tel: 081-993 7334

STN International
The Royal Society of Chemistry
Thomas Graham House
Milton Road
Cambridge CB4 4WF
Tel: 0223 420237

9 Select bibliography

Up to date information on environmental auditing and associated issues can be found in various printed sources. The following selected list has been compiled using the journals and databases covered in Chapter 8 Sources of Information on Environmental Auditing. It includes full details of all the references given in the book, as well as listing some items for further reading.

More detailed information on environmental information services can be found in *Environmental information: a guide to sources*, Nigel Lees and Helen Woolston, London: The British Library, 1992. ISBN 0712307834.

Copies of some of the articles listed below can be obtained by contacting the British Library's Environmental Information Service (071-323 7955).

The ALA Environment Charter: a green audit for London, London: Association of London Authorities, 1991

'B&Q cracks down on vendors' environmental audits', *National Home Center News,* March 2 1992, p60

British Standard 7750: environmental mangagement systems, Milton Keynes: British Standards Institution, 1992

'The changing attitude towards liability for damage to the environment under European Community law', J. Faulks, *European Environment,* June 1991, vol. 1(3), pp 17-20

Changing corporate values: a guide to social and environmental policy and practice in Britain's top companies, R. Adams et al. London: Kogan Page, 1991. ISBN 0749404108

'Clean-up costs force banks to rethink lending', Neil Bennett, *The Times,* 14 January 1992, p19

'Commission wins stronger powers to implement environmental policy', *EC Energy Monthly,* January 17 1992

Draft code of practice on environmental audits, Birmingham: Association of Environmental Consultancies, 1991

Environmental audit: a complete guide to undertaking an environmental audit for your business, Birmingham: HASTAM, 1991. ISBN 1852521007

The environmental audit: a green filter for company policies, plants, processes and products, John Elkington, Woking: Worldwide Fund for Nature, 1990

Environmental audit for local authorities: a guide, M. Jacobs, Luton: Local Government Management Board, 1991

Environmental audit handbook: basic principles of environmental compliance auditing, 2nd ed. Thomas H. Truitt et al. New York: Executive Enterprises Publications, 1983. ISBN 0880570237

Environmental auditing, edited transcripts from the CBI/ICC conference, 1990, London: CBI, 1990. ISBN 1871510171

'Environmental auditing: a consultant's eye view', Mark Hadley, *Environmental Protection Bulletin*, Issue 015, November 1991, pp3–6

Environmental auditing, ICC position paper on environmental auditing, International Chamber of Commerce, 1989. ISBN 9284210895

'Environmental auditing for industry: a European perspective', K. Clement, *European Environment*, June 1991, vol. 1(3) pp1–4

Environmental Auditing: fundamentals and techniques, J. Ladd Greeno et al, New York: Wiley, 1985. ISBN 0471819840

'Environmental auditing policy statement', *Environmental Protection Agency, Federal Register*, vol. 51, no. 131, 9 July 1986, pp 25004–25010

Environmental charter for local government, Duncan McClaren et al, London: Friends of the Earth, 1989

Environmental contacts: a guide for business, who does what in government departments, DTI, Issue No. 2, March 1992

'Environmental statements: guidance for review and audit', P. Tomlinson, *Planner*, 3 November 1989, vol 75(28), pp 12–15

Environmental Protection Act 1990: Waste Management, the Duty of Care: a Code of Practice, Department of the Environment, Scottish Office, Welsh Office, London: HMSO, 1991

'From environmental statement to audit', H. Lusser, *Housing and Planning Review*, Oct/Nov 1990, vol. 45(5), pp8–9

The green business guide: how to take up and profit from the environmental challenge, John Elkington et al. London: Gollancz, 1991. ISBN 0575046759

Greening the workplace: a TUC guide to environmental policies and issues at work, London: Trades Union Congress, 1991. ISBN 1850062234

'Industrial environmental auditing update', *Environment Business*, supplement, November 1991

Kirklees state of the environment report, Huddersfield: Kirklees Metropolitan Borough Council Department of Economic Development and Planning, 1989

'Making the case for environmental audits', *Process Engineering, Environmental Protection Supplement* number 3, 1991, pp11–13

Narrowing the gap: environmental auditing guidelines for business, London: Confederation of British Industry, 1990. ISBN 085201371X

Policy appraisal and the environment, London: Department of the Environment/HMSO, 1991

'Proposal for a council Regulation (EEC) allowing voluntary participation by companies in the industrial sector in a community eco-audit scheme', (92/C 76/02) COM (91)459 final, *Official Journal, Series C*, vol 76 (2), 27 March 1992

This green business: the impact of environmental issues on strategic management, C. Simms, Bradford: Horton Publishing Ltd, 1991

Your business and the environment: a DIY review for companies, London: Legal Studies and Services (Publishing) Ltd, 1991

Index

Printed by Hobbs the Printers of Southampton

ENVIRONMENTAL INFORMATION FOR BUSINESS

Keeping up with change

Working towards a better environment means keeping your organisation up to date with new regulations, clean technology and increasing competition. Finding the right answer is vital to success.

When you need to answer questions like...

- *What European emission standards must I work to?*

- *What are the Best Available Techniques for cleaning up my factory?*

- *Which companies make pollution control equipment?*

... Then the British Library Environmental Information Service will be able to supply you with the data and the documentation you need. You save on time and you have the confidence that a comprehensive search has been done.

Can we help you?

A call to the Environmental Information Service is the only call you need to connect you with all the services of The British Library and other information suppliers. The dedicated phone line puts you in touch with our information specialists for a speedy response to your enquiries.

An initial survey of your problem is undertaken free of charge. When your requirements are fully analysed, computer databases and literature collections are searched to discover the articles, regulations, patents or standards that will provide the answer for you. Photocopies are sent by fax or first class post.

We will give an estimate of the charges for the search before starting and confirm additional work as it proceeds. The Service is open to all and there is no membership or joining fee.

A quick, free enquiry service is available for any immediate questions that you have, especially for names and addresses, product suppliers or checks on literature references.

Who are we?

The British Library is one of the world's largest suppliers of scientific, technical and business information. With major literature collections covering all environmental issues, together with links to key government libraries and online computer databases, The British Library is uniquely placed to supply industrial and commercial demands.

To discuss your information needs call the Environment Information Service on 071-323 7955 between 9.30 and 17.00 Monday to Friday, or send a fax on 071-323 7954.

The world's leading resource for scholarship, research and innovation